The President of India, Pranab Mukherjee

Hon'ble Justice SH Kapadia, CJI, conducting oath of presidency on Pranab Mukherjee

Family members of President Pranab Mukherjee after his swearing-in ceremony at the Parliament

The President of India, Pranab Mukherjee, delivering his speech on assumption of office as the President of India in the Central Hall of Parliament on July 25, 2012.

The President of India, Pranab Mukherjee, receiving the National Salute from the President's Body Guard (PBG) at Parliament House on July 25, 2012.

On his way to Rashtrapati Bhawan: Thanking people.

Ceremonial Guard of Honour in Rashtrapati Bhawan

Pranab Mukherjee with Prime Minister Manmohan Singh, Congress President Sonia Gandhi and AK Antony

Pranab Mukherjee with top Congress leaders

The Governor of Meghalaya, Ranjit Shekhar Mooshahary calling on the President of India, Pranab Mukherjee, on July 26, 2012 to felicitate him on his assumption of office as the President of India.

The Chiefs of Defence Forces calling on the President of India, Pranab Mukherjee on August 7, 2012.

The President of India, Pranab Mukherjee, hosted 'At Home' to the Freedom Fighters on the occasion of the 70th anniversary of the Quit India Movement at Rashtrapati Bhavan on August 9, 2012.

Narendra Modi Chief Minister of Gujarat, calling on the President of India, Pranab Mukherjee at Rashtrapati Bhavan in New Delhi on August 18, 2012

The President of India, Shri Pranab Mukherjee, senior leader of BJP, Shri Lal Krishna Advani and his wife, Smt. Kamala Advani at the Ashoka Hall of Rashtrapati Bhavan during the Iftar Reception hosted by the President on 17 August, 2012.

The Chief of the Naval Staff, Admiral D.K. Joshi, PVSM, AVSM, YSM ,NM, VSM, ADC calling on the President of India, Pranab Mukherjee at Rashtrapati Bhavan in New Delhi on September 12, 2012

The President of India, Pranab Mukherjee, administering the oath of office to Justice Altamas Kabir, as Chief Justice of India at the swearing in ceremony at Rashtrapati Bhavan on September 29, 2012.

The President of India, Pranab Mukherjee visiting the Nishat Garden at Srinagar in Jammu and Kashmir on September 27, 2012. He accompanied by the Governor of Jammu and Kashmir, Shri N.N. Vohra and the Chief Minister Omar Abdullah

The President of India, Pranab Mukherjee meeting Air Force Officers at the 'At Home' function hosted by the Chief of Air Staff, Air Chief Marshal N.A.K. Browne in New Delhi on October 8, 2012.

The President of India, Pranab Mukherjee inaugurating the School Building of Mirati Junior High School at Mirati in West Bengal on October 21, 2012.

Pranab Mukherjee in Mirati during Durga Puja festival

The Union Finance Minister, Pranab Mukherjee arrives Parliament House to present the General Budget 2012-13, in New Delhi on March 16, 2012.

Indian Finance Minister Pranab Mukherjee (R) shakes hands with US Secretary of State Hillary Clinton prior to a meeting at the Cabinet Secretariat in New Delhi on July 19, 2011.

External Affairs Minister Pranab Mukherjee and a delegate with the US President George W Bush at the Oval Office, White House, in Washington

Former prime minister Indira Gandhi with the then finance minister Pranab Mukherjee in November 1982.

Pranab with his wife Subhra Mukherjee

Pranab Mukherjee with his daughter Sharmistha

President Pranab Mukherjee' son Abhijit Mukherjee flashes victory sign and shows the winning certificate to media after his win in Jangipur by-election in Murshidabad, West Bengal

Oh dear, this one is even bigger UPA presidential candidate Pranab Mukherjee is garlanded by Congress workers in Chennai.

No, no Kalash please UPA presidential candidate Pranab Mukherjee and Union Health Minister, Ghulam Nabi Azad during a meeting with Andhra Pradesh Chief Minister N Kiran Kumar Reddy in Hyderabad.

Poltu
to
President
Pranab Mukherjee

Attention Authors

Poltu
to
President
Pranab Mukherjee

Rajat Amarnath
(Senior Journalist)

Manas Publications
(We Convert Fighters into Writers)
New Delhi-110002 (INDIA)

MANAS PUBLICATIONS
(We Convert Fighters into Writers)
(Publishers, Library Suppliers, Importers & Exporters)
4402/5-A, Ansari Road (Opp HDFC Bank)
Darya Ganj, New Delhi-110 002 (India)
Off. ✆ 23260783, 23265523, Fax: 011-23272766
E-mail: manaspublications@vsnl.com
manaspublications@gmail.com

ISBN 978-81-7049-444-7
₹ 695/-

Designed at
Manas Publications

Printed in India at
RK Offset, Delhi
and published by Mrs Suman Lata for
Manas Publications, 4402/5-A,
Ansari Road (Opp HDFC Bank),
Darya Ganj, New Delhi-110002 (INDIA)

Contents

Preface

Pranab Mukherjee took the oath as the 13th President of the Sovereign Democratic Republic of India on 25th July, 2012. The success story of Pranab Mukherjee's life stands testimony to the merit and relevance of the very concept of India, and all the values that this great civilization stands for.

The selection process for the candidature for election of the 13th President was an unprecedented sequence of events, stretching over one full month. Finally, it culminated in the announcement on June 15, 2012, by the Congress Party President and UPA Chairperson Sonia Gandhi, that Pranab Mukherjee was their choice as the presidential candidate. Their party felt he would be a worthy successor to the out-going President Pratibha Devi Singh Patil.

Sonia Gandhi voiced her conviction that 'the country will be safe in Mukherjee's hands'.

This book on Pranab Mukherjee's journey that now ends at the *Rashtrapati Bhawan* is quite unusual because his humility and simplicity is almost self-effacing, and hence very little is known about his personal life, despite the fact that his achievements are stupendous. Consequently, for any book to do justice to Mukherjee's persona, one had to sieve through whatever material was available, research what others have said about him, and then sew the material into a story, as remarkable as the life of Pranab Mukherjee.

We sifted through material on Mukherjee's birthplace Mirati in West Bengal, to his student years, which stretched from his village school to Calcutta university, met his family members, friends, teachers and colleagues, for first hand information and of course researched his political life which spans over 40 eventful years.

The picture became somewhat clear; he is a man with rare determination and perseverance, a person with a humble background striving to excel, by the dint of sheer hard work and individual merit and his innate wisdom. He is very well respected within the party as well as in public life. National and international media often brand him as a number-crunching politician with a phenomenal memory and an unerring survival instinct.

Piyush, his elder brother, views his phenomenal achievements with great sense of pride. For Annapurna, his elder sister, he is more like a son. For the friends, this is one friendship they will cherish lifelong. For politicians he is a mentor and unmatched crisis manager. And for the top-brass of India Inc, he is the 'Chanakya' of Indian economy and polity, in the truest sense of the term. That is Pranab Mukherjee, the new President of India.

Friends and detractors both admit he is an idealist, the kind needed to bring in change. He is pure as crystal, and truthful beyond suspicion. A practical, but a seasoned statesman, he knows how to tweak and tamper with his ideas to suit the surroundings.

Most of our Presidents, like, Dr Rajendra Prasad, Dr Radhakrishnan, Dr Zakir Hussain, Dr R Venkataraman, and Dr Shankar Dayal Sharma were elected to the office on the strength of their outstanding contributions to the national developmental process. Pranab Mukherjee is all set to join their ranks.

At present the country is passing through complex and growing crisis: the crisis of self-inflicted wounds. The nexus of politicians-bureaucrats and industrialists has been exposed through Right to Information (RTI) Act and judicial activism. The vote bank politics has made coalition Governments dysfunctional and has led to a policy paralysis. Much needed economic reforms are in a limbo. Liberalisation of economy has in fact directly or indirectly contributed to the corrosion of our value system; the collapse of dharma. The concept of an inclusive growth of all sections of population propounded by founding fathers of the nation like Mahatma Gandhi has been forgotten. The rich have become richer and the poor, poorer. A nation that was founded on the glowing motto of *Satyameva Jayate* is sinking in the ocean of corruption. It is expected Pranab Mukherjee will help rediscover the lost wisdom and arrest the devaluation of this office and provide it dignity, by creating new convention, that might help the country take a big leap forward.

Drawing from the wisdom and perceptions of many great people of our country like Swami Vivekananda, Gurudev Rabindranath Tagore, Sri Aurobindo, Mahatma Gandhi, Pandit Jawaharlal Nehru, Raja Ram Mohan Roy and many others, President Pranab Mukherjee can trigger and ignite the minds of youth, creative writers, artists, scientists, social and political activists, with idealism and pragmatism, for that Second Cultural Renaissance. This could arrest the negative forces of callousness and corruption and generate a climate of compassion, love and understanding and the spirit of self-sacrifice. Our motto of *Satyameva Jayate* should be translated into action by our politicians, bureaucrats, industrialists and other people of the country. The people of India hope and believe President Pranab Mukherjee will show the way.

The man who could have been Prime Minister is now the President. Pranab Mukherjee, Union Finance Minister, shed the perpetual man in-waiting label on June 15, 2012 as Sonia Gandhi announced his candidature for the President.

July 25th, 2012 marked the beginning of his journey to Raisina Hills. Pranab Mukherjee had moved on, to be the first citizen of India. It was indeed his date with destiny. On the 60th anniversary of Parliament, he took oath as the 13th President of the Republic of India. Our country's term for President, who as head of the state occupies an exalted place in the constitutional scheme of governance, is *Rashtrapati*.

Role of the President

With India becoming a Republic on 26th January, 1950 and with the assumption of office of the President by Dr Rajendra Prasad, a new era was heralded. The occupant of the highest office of the land is also the custodian of the Constitution.

While the President's function as the protector and defender of the Constitution has been adequately highlighted, the role played by the President to serve and promote the well-being of the people of India has not received much attention.

It was former President KR Narayanan, who said that he had carefully read the oath taken by him, and understood that it provided a wider scope to play the role of a working president, functioning within the boundaries of the Constitution, as opposed to an executive president. Observing that the office of the president gives little direct power or influence to the incumbent to interfere in matters or to affect the course of events, he added, "There is a subtle influence of the office of the president on the executive and the other arms of the government, and on the public as a whole. It is a position which has to be used with a philosophy of indirect approach. There are one or two things which you can directly do, in very critical times. But, otherwise, this indirect influence that you can exercise on the affairs of the state is the most important role you can play. And, he can play it successfully, only if he, his ideas and his nature of functioning are seen by the public to be in tune with their standards... there must be some equation between the people and the president".

The first President, Dr Rajendra Prasad, understood that the people would expect a lot from an elected president. Therefore, he wrote with insight: "Whatever the strictly correct legal and constitutional position may be, there is no doubt that in the case of an elected president people do look upon him also as a person having some authority in the governance of the country, and he can justify his position only by tendering such advice and giving such suggestions as he considers necessary to the cabinet before it takes any decision. Once a decision has been taken, whether with or without his suggestions or even against his suggestions, he has to act according to that decision".

In the era of coalition politics and government, the role of the president is of critical nature. The provisions of the Constitution coupled with the precedents set by the successive presidents constitute the source of inspiration and guidance to the future presidents of our country.

President Pranab Mukherjee, well-known for his political acumen and astuteness, by virtue of his political foresight, his capacity of judging people and situations, his enthusiasm for doing what is right, as also his deep love for mankind will surely emerge as respectable statesman of national and international repute.

I am highly thankful to Shib Ram Roy, who, on my insistence, personally met a few of Pranab Mukherjee's close family members, friends, colleagues, college principal and associates to have a glimpse of his likes and dislikes since his childhood days. I am grateful to all those personalities, who spared their valuable time in providing the basics of the life of the President of India. Shib Ram Roy has also helped in collecting and compiling information from other sources and editing the language of the book, for which I am grateful to him.

New Delhi **Rajat Amarnath**

Chapter - I

Humble Beginning

Early Life

Mirati is a non-descript, calm and quiet village of Birbhum district in West Bengal. Situated just 200 km south west of Kolkata, it still retains its simple village charm; and resembles that old village look as it was 78 years ago. But, for the past few months, there was a sense of palpable excitement amongst the simple village folks and the exuberance was almost contagious. Even, the winds that swept through the lush green surroundings of Mirati, tried to linger and whisper to the people, as if it had a new story to tell; the captivating story of a young prodigy, who dreamt many dreams and aspired to reach out, and touch the stars in the sky, some day. This boy is today the President of our country, i.e., India. He is, Pranab Mukherjee, an astute politician, a role model teacher, a devoted father and a loving husband. A gifted speaker, and also labelled as an intellectual person, he had indeed, a varied and engaging political career.

Pranab Mukherjee belongs to a respectable Bengali Brahmin family. Born on 11th December, 1935 to Kamada Kinkar Mukherjee and Rajlaksmi Mukherjee, his father was a well-known freedom fighter, who spent more than ten years in British jails during the freedom movement. His father was an active member of Indian National Congress, a member of All India Congress Committee (AICC) and also, a member of West Bengal Legislative Council from 1952 to 1964. Since Kamada Kinker Mukherjee was in active politics, it was taken for granted by friends and family, that his son Pranab, would follow his father's footsteps and join active politics too. His mother Rajlakshmi Mukherjee who belonged to the Jessore Brahmin family, now in Bangladesh, was a very pious lady and devoted much of her time to charity work and devotion to God.

His Siblings

Pranab Mukherjee has two brothers and one sister. His elder brother Amiya has left for his heavenly abode. His next brother Piyush and sister Annapurna Bandopadhaya are still alive and reside near their ancestral village. His sister lives in Parota and brother in Bolepur. Pranab is the youngest child in his family.

Childhood Dreams

Pranab's mother used to call him 'Poltu' with affection, when he was a child and that is the name, he is still known by, in Mirati village.

As a child, while gazing at the star lit sky, Poltu's vivid imagination conjured up a string of thoughts; thoughts that conveyed to his young mind, that only the educated, big and rich people travelled round the world in planes, and lived a fruitful and engaging life. He promptly made up his mind that, one day he too would become an ambassador representing his country. It's true, that the dream of that little rustic village boy, may not have been fulfilled but he had taken a giant leap, when, much later in his life, he was appointed as the External Affairs Minister of the country. In that capacity, in the later part of his political career, he appointed many ambassadors representing India, to various countries in the world. And now he is the 'First Citizen' of the country and the Supreme Commander of the Armed

Forces of India. That indeed is an epic journey in a person's political career.

Primary Education

Poltu started his initial education at a primary school in his Mirati village. After his promotion from class one to two, the Head Master was dissatisfied with him for his irregular attendance. He decided to take a stern measure and rusticate him from the school. But since his father Kamada Kinker Mukherjee was a highly respected patriotic leader of his time, the Head Master decided to give him another chance. He quizzed Pranab with some tough questions; the right answers would allow him to continue his studies in the school. To the Head Master's surprise and delight, Pranab gave the right answers to all the questions asked. The satisfied Head Master was not only highly impressed, he even ensured that Poltu got promoted to class four. A double promotion! Then there was no looking back; Poltu, after this incident, did not need to tap the world on its shoulders, to get noticed. He saw to it, from then onwards, that his studies never get interrupted, for any lack of sincerity on his part, till he acquired a double postgraduate degree.

But from standard two, he was unhappy with the atmosphere of that place. His thirst for knowledge made him yearn for a better education. Even in his early days, he wanted an education which would allow his curiosity to be indulged in, and his inquisitive mind to be satisfied. That just wasn't happening in the village school. So, he made a determined effort and started persuading his parents to get him admitted to Kirnahar Shib Chandra Boys School which was at that time, quite famous for imparting good education. The Principal of Kirnahar Shib Chandra Boys School tried and tested Poltu's academic capability, and to see how strong his desire was to get admission in this new school, used the same tactics as Poltu's Head Master, in the previous school used. He told him, "If you give the correct answers to the questions asked, I will grant you direct admission to standard five".

Poltu had come fully prepared because he did not want to be caught off-guard and lose out on getting admitted to the school. His answers hit bull's eye and Poltu was delighted with that right response. His admission was assured immediately! He turned out to be a brilliant student and those formative years in a good school laid the foundations of a brilliant career, yet to come.

During his school days, Pranab Mukherjee did not show any signs of being a politician. He was a simple and a fun loving naive village boy. Like his peers, he did not focus on what he really wanted to do in his life. His jovial but sharp mind is demonstrated in the following incident.

He always made it a point, to save a part of the pocket money that he got from his mother and build it up further, for later use. Replying to a question, raised, on this topic he said in jest,

"Mother would ask me to go to the market to buy a certain amount of an item and after much calculation, give me the exact amount of money accordingly. I would buy a little less of the item and pocket the extra money for myself. That way the stockpile of my pocket money never seemed to dwindle".

And this is what he did for many years, whenever his mother asked him to do some shopping for her. His ever loving mother never reprimanded him for this mischievous behaviour, but his elder brother soon caught on to the act, and did not spare him.

Pranab Mukherjee spent almost 17 years of his life at his ancestral house at Mirati. While remembering Poltu's childhood days, Pranab Mukherjee's sister Annapurna Bandopadhya reminiscences that she was certain that one day 'greatness' would smile upon her endearing younger brother, but never had she imagined that he would reach the pristine height of being the 'first citizen' of the country.

Eighty-year-old Rama Rani Dasi looks ecstatic, while admiring her childhood friend, looking down at him from a photo printed on a calendar.

Dasi gushes and squeals in delight, "Just imagine, my Poltu, my friend from my village, has gone so far, in the journey of life. I bless him with all my heart and pray that he achieves even more".

Pranab Mukherjee's school documents are still carefully kept in the Mirati's village primary school. He has met all the expenditure of building one of the school blocks of this primary school, which has been named in fond memory of his late father, Kamada Kinkar Mukherjee. When the people of Mirati got to know, that Pranab Mukherjee was the chosen candidate for the Presidential post, and his chances were very bright to be elected, they started offering prayers to Lord Shiva on a daily basis. And of course their sincere prayers were answered. The Shiva temple at Mirati village has also been renovated by Pranab Mukherjee. The people of Mirati have high hopes that their prodigious son would show the path, to take their country, to even greater heights. And this would not be any less of an achievement for them. Both, the honour and pride, of having rubbed shoulders with the 13th President of India will be theirs too.

At the 117-year-old Kirnahar Shib Chandra High School, all the students were an excited lot. After all, the key contender for the presidential post was from their own school.

One young student proudly had said, "I will be very happy if he becomes President. I can then claim that I am studying in Pranab Mukherjee's school". Another student said, "He has come from such a small village and studied in this school and today he has become the President. I feel that if I put in my best effort, I will also become like him some day".

It's only people who touch young minds and inspire them, to try to do things they never thought they were capable of, can be called true role models. Poltu might have done just that.

In 1946, Poltu, then a student of Class 5, was still a quiet and reticent young boy, but his desire to discuss issues on any topic, was given a chance to be showcased, when some sensitive teachers, noticed, and recognised his debating skills. This school provided the right platform for oratory skills, to be honed and sharpened here.

His teacher Amar Nath Dutt, nostalgically remembered the effort Pranab made to reach school on time. He had to walk and wade through mud, slush and water, to reach school, especially in rainy season. A long stretch of five kilometers, it was. He would wear a "*gamcha*," while wading through the water, lest he soiled his school uniform. A gentle and kind teacher allowed him to change his school uniform, at his house. "Humble beginnings indeed," sighed Dutt.

College Life

Having completed his schooling from Kirnahar Shib Chandra Boys School with brilliant results, Poltu attended the Vidyasagar College at Suri (Birbhum) then affiliated to Calcutta University.

In Suri Vidyasagar College in 1952, he completed his Intermediate Science course with first division. He then switched to the Humanities stream (Bengali Honours) in the same institution and graduated in 1956. At the graduation level his subjects were Bengali, Additional Bengali, English and History.

Continuing his academic pursuit, he got the masters' degree in History from Calcutta University. He did MA (History) as a regular student and MA (Political Science) as a private candidate simultaneously in 1958.

He later got a degree in Law, from the University of Calcutta in 1962, and added another feather to his cap with D.Litt. (Honoris Causa) when he was awarded an honorary Doctor of Letters degree by the University of Wolverhampton. An honorary D.Litt by the Assam University was also given to him in March 2012.

College life provided Pranab ample opportunities to involve himself in active politics and to begin with, he became a leader of the students union. This phase in his life, served as a platform to sow the seeds of what was to become a successful political career later on.

When the Principal of the Suri Vidyasagar College in Suri, (Birbhum distt) Dr Laxmi Narayan Mandal was contacted, he gave an account of Poltu's college life in details. The ambience surrounding Suri is lush green and breathtaking. Situated in the eastern part of West Bengal it has a mining belt, in the small hills surrounding the area. Nature at its splendour best...Salubrious ambience; excellent for academic pursuits.

The modest and amiable Principal Dr Mandal looked elated when he said "It is a great matter of pride that an ex-student of this institution is going to occupy the highest office of the country".

Dr Mandal then elaborated on how Vidyasagar College was first established. At the time of World War II, in 1942, the College was decentralised into two divisions - Suri Vidyasagar College and Nawadeep Vidyasagar College. JK Choudhary was the first Principal of this college, who controlled both the branches from the Calcutta head office. Tribhunga Murari Mandal was deputed to look after the day-to-day affairs of the college as a Vice-Principal.

Dr Mandal continued, "Prof Arun Sen became the Principal of the College in 1950. A brilliant educationist, he raised the standard of the institution in many ways. He gave a lot of importance to academics, culture and sports. Till date this college has maintained its high standards". It was Poltu's good fortune that he found mentors in such devoted teachers.

"Pranab was not only a good student but pro-active too, in all extra-curricular activities; debating events saw him excel. Taking home the trophy had become a regular feature, giving him the confidence to become a gifted orator," added Dr Mandal.

Dr Mandal gave the reference of Dev Ranjan Mukhopadhya, Poltu's Bengali subject teacher, and Paresh

Nath Mandal an Advocate; Poltu's roommate at the time of his doing Law.

Before concluding, Dr Mandal added that ex-Olympian and great soccer player PK Banerjee and Tulsi Giri who became the Prime Minister and President of Nepal, were students of this college too.

When Pranab Mukherjee was the Deputy Chairman of the Planning Commission in 1996, he played a key role in getting about one crore grant from the Centre for this college. 'Arobindo Bhawan', another wing of this college, saw the light of the day, only because of this fund being offered by the government.

"Pranab Babu himself inaugurated it," said Dr Mandal with great pride.

Dr Mandal sighed deeply and said, "Once I did get a chance to meet Pranab Babu, at the golden jubilee celebrations of the college but I was so overwhelmed with his towering personality that I could not gather enough courage to state my request".

On meeting Prof Dev Ranjan Mukhopadhya, who used to teach Bengali in the College then, said, "No doubt Pranab was good student but not an outstanding one. He was an introvert, but a confident person who knew how to express what was on his mind. His love for Bengali literature saw him switching subjects, from science to Bengali".

Prof Mukhopadhya closed his eyes and thought for a second and then said, "Ah! Yes....I forgot to talk about his elephantine memory! His ability, every time to narrate facts vividly, recollecting the exact date and time of the events, in his own eloquent manner, never failed to impress me".

The octogenarian Prof Mukhopadhya carried on saying, "He was never satisfied with his academic performance. He always aimed higher. Though he scored the highest percentage among the nine students of his stream, including a girl, he felt he had fallen short of his own expectations. I consoled him, stressing on the fact that life ahead would offer him many more chances to excel".

This eighty-eight years old teacher further elaborated, "I saw shades of his excellent leadership qualities, even in those days. His participation in all cultural activities, displayed his excellent organising capabilities. In fact he was one of the favourite students of the then Principal Arun Sen, whom Pranab considers to be his ideal teacher".

On asking about Pranab's role in the students union, he added, "The students union, 'Chhatra Parishad', worked with enthusiasm and great zeal for the benefit of all students, especially the underprivileged ones, who needed the support of the union the most. Of course, Pranab's active participation, in the full time work of the union spearheaded the union in the right direction".

Advocate Paresh Nath Mandal recalls: "I first met Pranab Babu in 1959 when he was a law student in the University of Law, Calcutta. He was one year senior to me. Despite his best efforts, but much to his disappointment, he could not get a first division in Law, which he completed in 1962. But in those days, due to various constraints, a result in the first division never came easily to students".

"While doing his MA (History) in Calcutta University his role in student politics was not visible, but in the Law University, his interest in politics finally surfaced," said Paresh Nath Mandal.

"At the keenly contested college elections, he came out a winner and became the president of University College of Law Student Association (UCLSA). He defeated his nearest rival Harshit Ghosh from 'Chhatra Parishad' by a margin of just one vote! At that time Shymal Kumar Chaterjee - a good friend, also won the election as a general secretary. Shymal Kumar Chaterjee, was quite close to the then supremo of Bangla Congress, Atulya Ghosh," recollected Paresh Nath Mandal.

Dabbling in college campus politics and being in the fold of political people, paved the way for Pranab to join mainstream politics.

Paresh Nath Mandal confirmed that, "As an active student union leader, he always came forward, to help any student in distress. He played a key role in organising debates, music and dance competitions, mock parliament sessions, literary programmes and other sports and cultural activities in the college premises".

Advocate Mandal also certified his sharp memory. He said, "In 1964, when Jawaharlal Nehru passed away, an editorial was published in *The Statesman*. At a function, Pranab Da narrated the entire editorial, without missing out a single word. This of course got him the praise and applause, he so deserved for this exceptional memory skill".

During an interview Pranab Mukherjee in his own words said, "In 1948 when I was just 13 and studying in class seven, I stunned the District Magistrate visiting our school in Kirnahar village, by correctly naming the contestants in the US presidential elections which were being held that year. The District Magistrate (DM), PPI Baidanathan was an ICS officer. Before entering my classroom, he had asked the same question to students of classes 8, 9, and 10, i.e., to name the American presidential candidates. No student had a clue. To the delight of my Head Master, I told the DM that the incumbent Harry S Truman and his rival Thomas Dewey were in the race".

The District Magistrate eyes widened in amazement, he was totally stumped. The Head Master had to explain to the DM, "American elections were discussed at his home because his father was in active politics".

Paresh Nath Mandal stated that, "Even though Pranab Da had his own share of burdens, he would visit his Law college mess often, to meet me. At that time his family was settled at Kadamtala, Howrah. As his family was passing through financial constraints, he took up his first job in the office of the Deputy Accountant-General (Post and Telegraph) in Calcutta office to lessen the burden of his family. This does speak highly of his commitment to his family and compassion for fellow human beings".

Paresh Mandal further added, "When Pranab Babu joined politics, the Naxal movement was at its peak. Due to ideological differences, he could never support the Naxal cause. In any case, this movement's ideological value got diluted and lost its meaning mid-way, drawing criticism from all quarters. Eventually, this movement was subdued by the government".

Leadership Even as a Teenager

"During his nearly five decade old political career he has been praised as a great statesman and a leader. But let me state that he had started honing his skills as leader and as an orator since his school days," Mihir Chattopadhyay, Pranab's classmate in Kirnahar Shib Chandra High School, told that he was a close friend of Poltu till graduation. "The 76-year-old man, who retired as a teacher from his alma mater, recollected how in 1949 Poltu impressed and convinced a minister to renovate the school building.

"During those days, the country had just got freedom. Our school was in a very bad shape. There were no doors and windows, and just had a thatched roof. One day our Head Master told us that a senior minister would come to the school for inspection. The Head Master asked a few students of Class 9 and 10 to volunteer, to voice the school's problems before the minister," Mihir said.

Mihir continued "Most of the students were afraid to speak before the minister. But Pranab, though a student of class 7, decided to volunteer and present the case. With his oratory and reasoning skills and a persuasive bent of mind, he convinced the minister to help the school authorities in renovating the school. The minister was so impressed that he prophesied that Pranab Mukherjee would become someone big and famous in future".

Mihir remembered how Pranab had led a class boycott in protest against a false complaint against the students.

"We were then in class 9. One morning when we entered the classroom we found most of the furniture was broken. The Head Master, lost his cool, and alleged that we had done the damage. He ordered us to pay a fine".

"It was Pranab, who came to our rescue. He argued that the students should not be made to pay any fine as they have not broken the furniture. Under his leadership, we boycotted classes for the day. The Head Master later came and pacified us".

Mihir Chattopadhayay still remembers how the Head Master patted Pranab on the back and praised him for his leadership qualities and the conviction of his beliefs, "Till 1998 we were in regular touch," he said. The retired teacher wishes to meet his old friend, when he comes to Kolkata next, as the First citizen of the country.

Personal Life

Pranab Mukherjee tied the nuptial knot at the age of 22 when he had noticed a comely girl, named Subhra, who was not only a good singer but a painter too. He confided in his sister, who informed their parents and managed to persuade them too. The arranged marriage turned into a grand wedding ceremony on July 13, 1957.

Pranab Mukherjee has been married to Subhra Mukherjee for 55 years and has been blessed with two sons, Abhijit (now MP) and Indrajit and a daughter Sharmistha Mukherjee (Kathak dancer).

On being asked about wishing him, after Pranab Da became President, Subhra said, "No, no. We are not like today's couples. It's not a lovey-dovey relationship and we don't express our emotions overtly. It's all in the mind and heart. We rarely indulge in small love talk. At our age, it's more about depending on each other whole-heartedly. His love for me is different. Every day after his bath, he comes to me, touches my forehead and recites some '*mantras*'. He does this every day of the year and yesterday (July 23, 2012) was no exception. This is how he expresses his love.

We have been married for 55 years and we haven't fought for a single day".

Pranab's wife Subhra belongs to Narrail district of Bhadravila village which is now in Bangladesh. This village celebrated and distributed sweets when the news of Pranab Mukherjee's victory in the presidential election reached them. Subhra was born in Bhadravila village and spent a part of her childhood days in her home town. Pranab's brother-in-law Kanhai Lal Ghosh still lives in this village.

Kanhai Lal said that his sister Subhra, came to the village last in 1998 with her daughter Sharmistha.

Pranab's elder brother Piyush Mukherjee worked with the Centre for National Integration (Shantiniketan, Vishwabharati Vidyalaya). He retired as the director from the same institution. His brother and his wife now reside in Bolepur in West Bengal.

Piyush said that his brother Pranab had displayed good leadership qualities right from childhood. Even though he played truant from school sometimes, he still managed to fare well in his academics. Maybe that was the reason his teachers and other family members overlooked his flaws, and still showered affection and praise on him.

Dada has a Sweet Tooth

Confirming that Pranab Da has a sweet tooth, Pradyut Guha, Pranab Mukherjee's personal assistant since the last eight years and one of his most loyal disciples says, "He simply loves his sweets. Moderately diabetic, he does indulge once in a while, in eating them. He loves chocolates and *rasogollas*. In fact he is familiar with most of the local sweet shops in every district, he travels in West Bengal. He relishes his favourite '*ladykini*' (a fried sweet made of curd and semolina) after all meals. Whether Mukherjee will offer tea and sweets at Rashtrapati Bhavan remains an open question!

Though a non-vegetarian, he likes simple food like soups and juices. Subhra Mukherjee, further adds that her husband's favourite dishes are *aloo posto* (Potato and *ground poppy seeds*) and *jhinge posto* (Prawns and *ground poppy seeds*) apart from rice and fish curry. "I would have loved to cook these dishes for him, but my ill-health prevents me from doing so," she said. Pranab's son Abhijit added that apart from chocolates, his all time favourite, he has a great fascination for Alphonso and Himsagar mangoes.

His sister Annapurna elaborated further, "Pranab is fond of vegetable dishes such as 'mochar ghonto' (minced and spiced banana cone cooked dry), 'shukto' (bitter mixed vegetable curry), and 'danta chachhari (dry dish of drumsticks and spinach stalks). He is also fond of cooking".

An Interesting Tale

Pranab's younger days which are lessons in themselves, tell many a tale, reflecting the person he is; austere, humble and committed. One such tale is about how a lunch costing just 56 *paise* was enough to keep him going for the whole day! He would take one or two classes in the morning, eat at *'Rakhalda's'* canteen -- a sumptuous lunch of dal, egg, and rice. Opt for *'aloo bhaja'* (fried potato chips) instead of chutney (as sweet tomato preparation in Bengali cuisine). Take his afternoon nap, a practice since then, before he headed for Kolkata, by 4 pm for some political activity.

His Daily Routine

An early riser, he is up at dawn by 5 am and then spends at least an hour for his walk and exercise. Over four cups of tea, he gets his daily dose of news from at least four newspapers, reading carefully from beginning to end. After a shower, he unfailingly does his 'puja' for about 40 minutes. Though not a fanatic, he is religious and believes in rituals and is a devotee of Chandi Mata (Ma Durga). After that it is breakfast time for him.

His Recreation Time

"Being always on the move, he hardly gets time to indulge in any major hobby or recreation, but his jovial nature sees him quite often cracking jokes with his family members. At times he even calls his friends by different nicknames. "He calls me '*Padda*' in jest and that never fails to bring a smile on my lips!" said Pradyut Guha.

"His major entertainment is talking to people, his family and friends. We Bengalis may have a simple meal on weekdays, but on Sundays we love eating meat curry, fish and rice with the family. Pranab Da, also, unwinds on Sunday, in a similar manner. He knows the best way to rejuvenate is to be in touch with one's family and friends. Showing no craving for modern day cell phones, even though he carries one around, he keeps phone conversations to the minimum," Pradyut Guha continued.

What He Reads

Reading remains his favourite past time, in fact it wouldn't be wrong to say that books are his best friend. He reads a little every night and he is very often found asleep, with a half open book on his lap. His son says that he prefers to read books, related to political science. Historical books and fictions fascinate him too. The books of Sarat Babu, Bankim Chandra, Rabindranath Tagore, Tarashanker Bandopadhyaya and Vidysagar are his all time favourites. He is known to be a voracious reader and he usually reads three books simultaneously. During the Presidential polls in 2012, he was reading, "*Confrontations that shaped a nation*'. Some of the confrontations are romantic like the one between Antonio and Cleopatra. The book discusses the crisis after the Second World War and just before the cold war" he said in an interview with the magazine *The Week* (August 5, 2012). Being an avid reader of Indian and world history, the era that excites him the most is World War II. He is inspired by Chinese politician Deng Xiaoping. Not being computer-friendly, he does not surf the net.

He has been writing a diary for the past 40 years to record in a chronicle, everything he's seen in his life but apparently these writings will be published by his daughter Sharmistha, only posthumously.

Once Pranab Da jokingly said, "I became pro-development, when I kept books on my head and waded across the river to reach my school. I thought silently, if ever I get an opportunity, I will build a *'pucca'* road to my school. How I wished I could ride a bicycle to school then".

Fond of Music

Strains of *'Rabindra Sangeet'* (songs written and set to tune by Rabindranath Tagore) is heard very often from his house. He listens to *Rabindra Sangeet*, every night before going to sleep. The present West Bengal Chief Minister Mamata Banerjee presented a special set of Tagore's songs recently to him.

Stress on Fitness

Pranab Mukherjee likes to remain 'fighting fit'. Apart from badminton, the game of football also holds his interest. At University level, he was the college champion in badminton. Till about 10 years back, he had a badminton court in his house where he would play regularly.

In a recent interview, he said that he loves to walk in the morning, adding, "I take 40 rounds of my lawn measuring 90 metres, which makes about three-and-a-half kilometers".

"Fluent in Bengali and English, his Bengali looks is evident in his style of dressing and his habits. He still calls his barber home! I can't imagine Pranab Mukherjee without his *'dhoti.'* Pranab Da has decided to wear the *'dhoti'* during his stay at Rashtrapati Bhavan too," says Pradyut Guha.

His mentor was Indira Gandhi and he believes in the Indian philosophy. He has two sons and a daughter and they all hold a special place in his heart. His daughter is very close to him whom he affectionately calls 'Munni', added Pradyut Guha.

Chapter - II

Poltu Does Mirati Proud

Mirati's Elated Inhabitants

Ever since Pranab Mukherjee's nomination as the UPA's presidential candidate was announced, the joy of the simple but enthusiastic village folks of Mirati, including his family members and relatives, knew no bounds. Their hearts swelled in pride, just thinking that a sincere and humble man, hailing from their village was expected to walk into the spacious Rashtrapati Bhavan as the 13th President of the second largest democracy in the world. Elation and a celebratory mood seemed to continue in the village and the primary school at Mirati for days together. The would-be first citizen's name was on everyone's lips. The people of Mirati were certain that their very own 'Poltu', the seasoned politician, well-versed with rules of his country's Constitution, will prove his credibility by discharging his duties with maturity. They staunchly believe that Poltu clearly understands the job of the President is to protect, preserve and defend the Constitution of the country. Poltu being the first Bengali President of India, their happiness is even sweeter now.

Mirati's Soil always Enticed Poltu

This is an amusing incident which took place in 1999. As usual, Pranab Babu came to visit his home town Kolkata en route to Mirati during the Durga puja festival. In his jovial mood he told the journalists who had come to interview him, as to why he could never aspire to be the prime minister of the country or the chief minister of West Bengal. Smiling he gave the three reasons:

"First, I cannot speak fluent Hindi. Second, like Nehru, Indira Gandhi, Atal Behari Vajpayee, Jyoti Basu, Rajiv Gandhi and Mamata Banerjee, I am not a mass leader. Third, I do not have a charismatic personality like them nor can I give inspiring speeches like them".

Amused, the mediamen asked, "then what is so special about you?" Pranab Babu said, "I was a student of Indian politics, and hence I understand Indian and world history thoroughly. I also have an uncanny ability to assess the future, keeping the present situations in mind. It's my lifelong dream of getting the job of the highest constitutional post (President) of India one day".

Even after becoming President in 2012, he celebrated Durga Puja festival in his village with his family and friends.

Lifelong Aspiration to Become the President

Now who can say dreams don't come true? It's debatable whether his lifelong aspiration to become the President of India was true or not. But Pranab Babu's elder sister Annapurna Bandopadhaya, has a logical conclusion to corroborate this fact.

Annapurna reveals "This story was set in 1969. Pranab was elected as a Rajya Sabha member on the ticket of Bangla Congress, for the first time and was allotted a Bungalow at Delhi's South Avenue. The President's Estate was quite near to Pranab's residence and from the verandah of the Bungalow, clearly visible, was the stable of President's Estate; so were the beautiful and strapping white horses of Raisina Hills. Seeing the special treatment and extraordinary care the horses got at the stables, in a lighter vein, Pranab remarked, "Just look Didi at the care those horses get! I would prefer to be the President's Estate buggy horse in my next birth".

Annapurna's total belief in her brother's greatness, made her say, emphatically, "Why just a horse, God willing, you will become the President of India and that too in this very birth". With a twinkle in his eye and a hearty laugh, Poltu said, "It is not so easy, Didi".

True that Pranab Mukherjee belonged to a political family and his father Kamada Kinkar was in the Indian National Congress, who served the Congress party in various positions in state and national politics. But Pranab Da's journey in politics was not started at the behest of his father.

Introduction to Politics

It all started with Pranab Mukherjee being introduced to Surendra Mohan Ghosh. Referred to as Dada, SM Ghosh was also Indira Gandhi's political mentor.

Whenever Ajoy Mukherji, president of Bangla Congress and later Chief Minister of Bengal in the joint Left Front government in 1969, was in Delhi, he would make it a point to see SM Ghosh at his residence on 21 Janpath. Ajoy Mukherjee when first introduced to Pranab Da at SM Ghosh's house, learnt that Pranab's father had the distinction of working with SM Ghosh, when he was the President of Bengal Pradesh Congress, in the late thirties. Pranab Babu's father Kamada Kinkar was a freedom fighter and after independence, he was elected as Member of the Legislative Council and kept this post for ten long years.

SM Ghosh had realised that Pranab Mukherjee had inherited politics in his genes and that he understood Sri Aurobindo's message in totality, that India's civilization was based on harmony of various religious traditions, capacity of assimilation and absorption, universality of spirit, pluralism and tolerance, dignity and divinity of the individual. SM Ghosh even mentioned this admirable facet of Pranab's personality to Indira Gandhi and very often emphasised that Pranab would play a crucial role in shaping the destiny of the country; from the ethical and spiritual perspective.

Thus it was Ajoy Mukherjee who introduced Pranab to politics in 1960 and was his mentor during his early political life.

Pranab Da's son Abhijit, further told "When any function was organised at Kiranhar High School and any big stalwart would visit the school to attend a function, his grandfather was also invited being a respected person of that area. Once at a similar function held at Kirnahar High School, a minister was invited along with his grand-father, Kamada Kinkar Mukherjee. His grand-mother (Rajlakshmi) asked Pranab's elder brother, Piyush to take care of him, so that he would not go to the function. But both the brothers disobeyed their mother and went to the school function, just out of curiosity, and that too, without their shirts! But their father's keen eyes spotted them in the crowds and reprimanded them at home, later. This same fun loving and carefree Poltu did every one proud by becoming a Union Minister in Indira Gandhi's Cabinet in 1973. And now, he has become the President of India".

As a Finance Minister, Pranab Mukherjee visited his ancestral home, when he was nominated for the presidential candidate. He tells everyone, that, "I am a simple village folk. The natural beauty of villages and simple life of the villagers always attracts me". When he reached his village, the melodious sound of conch shells and rhythmic drum beats, welcomed him. His ancestral home has a temple where the statues of *Radha-Krishna* and goddess *Ma Durga* are installed. This serene and pious atmosphere, never fails to rejuvenate him, he said, and he feels he can drop the cloak of worries of his urban life and distress here with great ease.

Fulfilling a Promise Made to Himself

The road leading from the village to the school has been named as Kamada Kinkar Mukhopadhay Sarani. Two years ago, he finally got a chance to fulfill that wish he had made to himself while wading through the water to go to school. A *pucca* road now stretches from his village to his school at Kirnahar. It was built by the Central government and is named after his father.

When asked whether he would like to visit his village after becoming the President? With a smile, his voice echoing with pride, he said, "I will never miss that chance".

Flood-Affected Mirati

Pranab's village Mirati is in a flood-affected area. Every year during the monsoon season, it is submerged due to flood water from Kuniye River. Possibly, from now on it might not happen, as his MLA son Abhijit had got a barrage erected to stop the flood waters from entering the village. It has been built this year, by a fund of 4.83 crore granted from the Central government.

Pranab's boyhood playmate Baldev Roy admitted that, "Pranab's son has done this good gesture to help the villagers overcome the grief they face, due to the flood waters entering their village each year during rainy season. Of course it will help his son win the hearts of the villagers and give a boost to his political career in the bargain".

At the twilight of his political career, Pranab has put the responsibility of carrying the reign of his political legacy on his son's shoulder. It is expected that his son Abhijit would also rise to the occasion to justify his father's faith. Of course, he will get necessary guidance to join the mainstream politics from his father.

Unique Bonds with Mirati

When Poltu came to his ancestral village recently, all his school and childhood playmates got together to meet him. His old pals of 'Lovpur Brahmanpara' Primary School narrated the past incidents related to Poltu, to their grand children. Among Poltu's friends, Sabita Rani Mazumdar was the naughtiest of the lot. She had plenty of stories to narrate. While reminiscing her childhood days, she told everyone that Poltu and all others would play in the mud all day long and run 'with the wind' on their way to school. She revealed that though Poltu was admired for his sharp mind, he was cranky and quarrelled very often with his friends. That is why they called him '*pala*' and how he hated this teasing term.

According to Sabita Rani, "Poltu got the highest rank from Birbhum district in class four scholarship examinations, but the Head Master of the school punished him for his bad and ineligible hand writing, which remains the same till date".

"Swimming in the river Kuniye was very popular with the children, and everyone wore the *gamcha* (thin towel). Taking care of the *gamchas* was Laxman Mandal's job. Eighty-five years old Laxman Mandal still runs his father's shop where, on their way to school, Poltu and his friends kept the *gamchas* for safe keeping. "Now, it is difficult to even meet Poltu, for security reasons," said Sabita Rani.

Sabita Rani continued, "When Poltu became Union Minister for the first time in 1973, he visited Mirati as usual to seek the blessings of his parents, seniors and relatives. On Poltu's invitation, Bindu, Ghudu, Shanti and I got together to meet him".

She said "All of us still remember the time we went to the village fair, without informing our parents. All daylong we loitered in the fair, running around and climbing trees. We got down on our knees and made mud houses with palm leaf thatched roofs. We even kept stones, sand and vermilion inside those houses as if conducting a *puja* ceremony. Bread and *batasha* were kept in those mud houses as *prasad*, which very often the stray dogs stole and ate! Poltu would be livid seeing that, he blamed us for not keeping guard over those little mud houses. How we fought with each other over trivial issues! Of course we all got our clothes dirty because our hands and feet were caked with wet mud; but as children we did not have a care in the world. Childhood innocence has its own charm, I guess".

Baldev Roy, Poltu's school mate, remembered how Poltu promised to speak, only in English to all his friends after passing class 10, and he did so, much to the amusement of all his friends. "He tried his best, but his accent remained as 'Bengali' as it is today," they laughed.

His sister Annapurna recalls "Poltu was also very disobedient. He did not like to go to the village primary school when he was a child. One day, he had beaten his servant who escorted him to the village primary school, and disappeared for the whole day. There was utter chaos trying to locate him. Later my mother reprimanded him severely".

A farmer named Biswajit Mandal, who still resides adjacent to Mukherjee Babu's village house, says, "Pranab Babu would visit Mirati each year, without fail, for the grand Durga Puja celebration and would spend those days with all his classmates, old friends and relatives. His 'morning walks' gave us access to him when he would inquire about our welfare. He stayed, as always, in his sister Annapurna's house at Parota for the night. One chamber was always kept reserved for him in his sister's house. A table and a chair was a must, to cater to his habit of reading late into the night".

Two of his classmates Mihir Chatterjee and Baldev Roy revealed that Pranab developed his reading habit to such an extent, that he even made a small library in his own room.

Annapurna revealed, "His favourite song is '*Abak Prithivi Tomai Salam*' (Oh! Strange world, I salute you), written by the famous poet of Bengal, Sukanta Bhattacharya, sung by Hemant Mukherjee. He still used to sing this favourite song of his".

Sharp Mind

"He has got a razor sharp brain and wit and humor are a part of his nature. All the workers and leaders in the Congress party, hold him in high esteem and say that Pranab Da is a walking 'encyclopaedia'. They said that his mind is as sharp as that of *Chacha Choudhary*, the comic character.

He still reads the comics of *Chacha Choudhary* in his spare time", said Annapurna with a smile.

Obstinate Pranab

Today's calm and composed Pranab Da was quite obstinate in his early life. His brother Piyush narrated the incident of changing schools and getting admission in class five, as a sign of how headstrong and determined he could be. The interesting thing was that at that time his sister Annapurna, who was six years older than him, was studying in class six.

Piyush Mukherjee further adds that, "History was the favourite subject of Pranab. The Japeshwar Mahadev Mandir built in 580-625 AD, by famous King Raja Sashanka, was near our ancestral village Mirati. In 1999, Pranab rebuilt the dilapidated temple by spending more than Rs one crore and also made a trust in his mother Rajlakshmi Devi's name, to take care of the temple".

The chairman of the trust Ravi Chatterjee explained, "The King Sashanka's capital was in 'Karnasubarna' (now in Murshidabad district), later the King transferred his capital to 'Gaud' (now in Malda district)". The interesting point is that Pranab Mukherjee was elected as an MP from both these places.

Spiritually Inclined

Abhijit said, "During Durga Puja, though Bipadtaran Bandopadhyay of Brahmanpara, was our family priest, my father made it a habit of chanting *Chandipath,* during the *Pujas*, in Sanskrit, a language he knows well".

Pranab's elder sister Annapurna elaborates, "During *Nabanna Puja* (the festival of eating newly-grown rice in autumn), Pranab would carefully observe how our father conducted the rituals and imitate all that he had observed, by keeping the deity in a makeshift room with bamboo twigs and stone. Pranab Mukherjee comes to Mirati every year for the annual Durga Puja and dons the priest's robe for four days".

He has firm faith in Goddess *Ma Durga*. He observes fasts during the first three days of the Durga Puja. For Mukherjee, offering obeisance to *Ma Durga* during Durga Puja cannot be compromised. He even deferred the signing of the Indo-US civil nuclear agreement with US secretary of state Condoleeza Rice by a week, because he had to go to his village for Durga Puja celebrations.

His sister Annapurna says, "Despite his stern image in public life, my brother is fun-loving and a good company to children. He plays with my grand-daughters, jokes, teases them a little, recites poems and sings with them too".

Though she was not in a position to go to Delhi and attend her brother's swearing-in ceremony on 25th July, 2012, she waits for his next visit. "When I talk to him, I'll ask him to pay a visit. But even if I don't tell him, I know he will come here to seek my blessings", she said.

When asked whether she planned to give him any gift, she said, "What can I give him? The entire nation is giving him gifts. I will give him my blessings and love".

Pranab Mukherjee sponsors a football tournament every year 'Kamada Kinkar Gold Cup' named after his father in his electoral district of Murshidabad.

In October 2010, he was quoted as saying, "We never go on a holiday, except to meet family and friends during Durga Puja".

Plight of Rural People

Pranab Mukherjee understands the plight of the poor rural people because he has experienced it himself. He can understand the challenges that the common man faces, so he tries to find political solutions that can work in favour of the poorer section.

That explains Pranab Mukherjee's immediate focus on carrying forward the ongoing process of economic reforms in India, but with a human touch, to uplift the standard of downtrodden and poor village farmers and artisans. He abhors programmes that cause disruption in the lives of the poor, in the name of economic reforms. He wishes to link economic reforms with its benefits reaching to the deprived sections of the society, and make national growth all inclusive.

His first-hand experiences in Mirati have provided him a training ground to be an able administrator, a multi-faceted personality and a successful politician.

It is expected that this soft spoken, genial Bengali from Mirati who is a quintessential Congressman, will write a new chapter in making a huge transformation in the society, as President, like his earlier predecessors.

Sharmistha Mukherjee, Pranab Da's daughter said on July 22, 2012 after her father's landslide victory in the presidential election that, "My father, would give a new dimension to the office of President of India by utilizing his vast experience and his personal rapport with political leaders that cut across party lines". According to her, "My father has done justice to all the different offices he has held so far. He has fulfilled his duties and responsibilities to the best of his ability in whatever he has done".

Pranab Mukherjee's wife Subhra says "It's the crowning moment of her husband's political career, but she was happy to be at home as people celebrated his victory as India's first Bengali president".

"My mother and in-laws would have been happy to see him as President. But their blessings are with him. Both would have been over the moon if they were alive to see all this today. Moreover, his mentor Indira Gandhi would also have been happy for him", said Subhra nostalgically.

After his father romped home as India's 13th President, defeating former Lok Sabha speaker PA Sangma on July 23, 2012, securing almost 70 per cent of the vote to ensure his journey to Rashtrapati Bhavan, his son Abhijit said, "He never discussed whether he thought of becoming president or prime minister. He never discussed his future. He always said that he wanted to perform to the best of his ability".

Two Presidents: Two Countries

Now that Pranab Mukherjee is President, Birbhum would've given India and Bangladesh a president each. Earlier Abdul Sattar (born in Dakar village) had been the President of Bangladesh from 1981 to 1982. During partition he had chosen to go to Dhaka and later became a judge at East Pakistan's Supreme Court and Chief Election Commissioner.

Human Nature

This happened back in the winters of 1988, when Pranab had quit Congress due to differences with Rajiv Gandhi. On his return trip from a visit to 'Pushkar' in Rajasthan, his car hit a cyclist. Pranab Da immediately stopped his car and got down to see the injured cyclist.

No sooner had he got down, angry local villagers gathered around his car. Worse, the cyclist turned out to be a son of the village headman. The angry mob pelted stones at his car. Unable to speak Hindi; the language barrier hampered Pranab Da's chances of pacifying the irate crowd. He brought down tempers by telling people that it was important to give medical help to the injured person first.

The villagers agreed to let the car's driver take the injured cyclist to a nearby hospital, but they refused to let Dada budge from the accident spot, lest he ran away. Pranab then had to sit on a *charpoy* by the highway, while hundreds of stick-wielding villagers surrounded him. Later he accompanied some villagers to the hospital, enquired about the injured man, paid for his treatment and even bought him a new cycle.

Chapter - III

Professional & Political Career

Pranab Mukherjee started his career as an upper-division clerk in the office of the Deputy Accountant-General (Post and Telegraph) in Kolkata in 1957.

Unhappy with his job because the salary was not enough to meet his family's expenses, he quit the job. Getting no job satisfaction from this profession, Pranab Da resigned from the office of the Post and Telegraph and joined Vidyanagar College in South 24-Parganas, a district of West Bengal, as a lecturer in 1963. He lectured on Indian politics, Indian Constitution and foreign constitutions. He became a member of the governing body of the college and its vice-principal in 1965. Failing to derive any pleasure from this job too, his inner voice compelled him to feel that this was not his true calling; he felt he could rise even more.

He compared his job as a teacher with that of a journalist and worked for the famous Bengali publication *Desher Dak* (Call of Motherland). He also became a trustee of *Bangiya Sahitya Parishad* and later President of *Nikhil Bharat Banga Sahitya Sammelan*.

His journalistic traits did show up for some time, when he contributed a few articles in some newspapers, but his leaning towards politics, weaned him away from choosing journalism as a profession. It was during his university days while studying law, that his real interest for active politics was noticed, and he became the general secretary of Bangla Congress.

Reminiscences of Pranab's Yesteryear Colleagues

When Pranab Mukherjee was sworn in as the 13th President, old friends from Bengal recalled with nostalgia the days spent with him in his early days.

Mahadev Sinha, the Principal of Bidyanagar College, South 24-Parganas district said that their friendship never waned, though Pranab Babu quit college in 1968, to join as a member of Bangla Congress. To him and a few others like Prodyut Kumar Mondal, now a retired professor of the college, "Pranab Mukherjee is but a phone call away".

"He spoke to us even when he was contesting the Presidential poll. He is still keen to know even small details about the college", they noted.

"Despite his high rank and stature he remains the simple man that he was. He shares '*telebhaja*' (deep fried vegetables), and '*muri*' (puffed rice) with us, which are amongst his favourite snacks," said Mahadev Sinha. He recalled the time spent on having the ever famous Bengali '*addas*' with them, during his visits to Kolkata. "Mangoes are his other weakness" they all recollected. "Pranab Babu as a teacher had an excellent rapport with the students. His amicable behaviour and his punctuality went down well with them," says former student Sunil Gorai, who later became the librarian of the college. "During his stay here, on weekends, Pranab Babu would go to a library on wheels, near his village. He took the cause of spreading education so seriously, that he made the entries in the book register in his own hand, so as to create a wide readership. After classes, he would train teachers of nearby Bidyanagar primary school," Gorai added.

Harendranath Majumdar, who was a minister in the Bangla Congress regime in the state, during the 1960s, had spotted Pranab Babu at the Bharat Sabha Hall Library. He had got him the job of a lecturer at the college, where he was the governing body president. Majumdar too had helped Pranab join politics in 1966 and the rest, as they say, is history.

Politics Beckons Pranab

A strange restlessness forced Pranab Da to change his jobs frequently. He felt he was destined for bigger things in life. Little wonder that one fine morning he left his job to take a plunge into politics and contest election. This decision stemmed from his anguish over the denial of political recognition and a party ticket to his father. Like all long journeys that must begin with that first step, this was possibly the first step in Pranab Da's long political sojourn.

His journey in the world of Indian politics has been full of ups and downs. Interestingly, while the number 13 may be perceived to be the unlucky number for most others, for him, this number brought luck. Possibly a sign, that this man was different from the rest. According to Hindu scriptures, 13 is the most auspicious number in Hindu calendar, it means '*tryodoshi*'. It is known that if anybody does something on this day, he will surely get a good dividend. It has proved right, in case of Pranab Da.

Lucky No 13 for 13th President Pranab Mukherjee

- Official residence before becoming the President: 13 Talkatora Road
- Office in Parliament House: Room no. 13.
- Date of marriage: 13th July, 1957.
- Oath as Member of Parliament for the first time: 13th July, 1969.
- First elected to Lok Sabha: 13th May, 2004
- Digits of the telephone number at his Kolkata residence add up to: 39 (3x13).
- His current dream run in the power corridor started after the 13th Lok Sabha.

- This number figures in the votes he received this Presidential election: 7,**13**,763

Bangla Congress

Congress in West Bengal, then was in the iron grip of Atulya Ghosh, an authoritarian party boss who would have been perfectly at home in the Tammany Hall. At one stage, he expelled from the party a respected leader, Ajoy Mukherjee, whose only fault was to insist on inner-party democracy. Ajoy Babu formed a new party, Bangla Congress with Sushil Dhara. Pranab Mukherjee threw his lot with this new party, soon becoming its General Secretary.

In 1967 and then in 1969, Ajoy Babu nominally led two short lived United Front governments in West Bengal that were actually dominated by the Communist Party of India (Marxist). Jyoti Basu was the Deputy Chief Minister.

During this time in July 1969, Pranab Mukherjee was first elected to the Rajya Sabha on the Bangla Congress' ticket. New Delhi at that time was in the throes of an intense power struggle between Indira Gandhi and a 'syndicate' of party bosses, of which Atulya Ghosh, the Congress boss from Bengal, was a member.

In Mainstream Politics

Seventy-seven years old, Mukherjee is a man of unparalleled experience in governance with the rare distinction of having served at different times as Foreign, Defence, Commerce and Finance Minister. He was elected to the Upper House of the Parliament (Rajya Sabha) five times from 1969 and twice to the Lower House of the Parliament (Lok Sabha) from 2004. He was a member of the Congress Working Committee, the highest policy making body of the Party for a period of 23 years.

During the period of 2004-2012, Mukherjee was instrumental in implementing critical decisions of the Government on a range of issues such as administrative reforms, Right to Information, Right to Employment,

Food Security, Energy Security, Information Technology and telecommunication, setting up of UIDAI, Metro Rail etc through Chairmanship of over 95 Groups of Ministers constituted for the purpose. In seventies and eighties, he was instrumental in setting up the Regional Rural Banks (1975) and the EXIM Bank of India as well as National Bank for Agriculture and Rural Development (1981-82). He was also author of a modified formula for resource sharing between the Centre and the States in 1991 which came to be known as the Gadgil-Mukherjee formula.

A powerful orator and scholar, Mukherjee's intellectual and political prowess as well as remarkable knowledge of international relations, financial affairs and parliamentary process are widely admired. He has been acclaimed for his role as a consensus builder on difficult national issues through his ability to forge unity amongst the diverse political parties that form part of India's vibrant multi-party democracy.

Under the careful mentoring of late Prime Minister Indira Gandhi, Mukherjee's rise in his political career was rapid. He was made Deputy Minister, Industry; Shipping and Transport, Steel and Industry and Minister of State for Finance in the period 1973-74. He assumed office as Finance Minister of India for the first time in 1982 in the Cabinet of Prime Minister Indira Gandhi and was Leader of the House in the Upper House of Parliament (Rajya Sabha) from 1980 to 1985. Later, he was Deputy Chairman of the Planning Commission from 1991 to 1996, Minister for Commerce from 1993 to 1995, Minister of External Affairs from 1995 to 1996, Minister of Defence from 2004 to 2006 and once again the Minister of External Affairs from 2006 to 2009. He was the Minister of Finance from 2009 to 2012 and Leader of the Lower House of Parliament from 2004 to 2012 till he resigned to contest election to the office of the President.

Mukherjee has extensive diplomatic experience and has served on the Board of Governors of the IMF, World Bank, Asian Development Bank and African Development Bank. He has led the Indian delegations to the Commonwealth

Finance Ministers' Conferences in 1982, 1983 and 1984; the United Nations General Assembly in 1994, 1995, 2005 and 2006, the Conference of Commonwealth Heads of Government at Auckland in 1995, the Non-Aligned Foreign Minister's Conference at Cartagena in 1995 and the Conference to mark the 40th anniversary of the Afro -Asian Conference in Bandung in 1995.

A voracious reader, Mukherjee has authored several books on the Indian Economy and on Nation Building. The many awards and honours conferred on him include India's second highest civilian award, Padma Vibhusan in 2008, the Best Parliamentarian Award in 1997 and Best Administrator in India Award in 2011. He was rated one of the best five Finance Ministers of the world in 1984 according to a survey conducted by "*Euro Money*" Journal published from New York and was declared 'Finance Minister of the year' for Asia in 2010 by "*Emerging Markets*", the journal of record for the World Bank and the IMF.

Catching Indira's Eyes

In 1969, Pranab Mukherjee was among the Rajya Sabha back benchers. His second speech in the House was on bank nationalisation and he was the last to speak. As he spoke, an impressed Indira Gandhi asked the then chief whip, who this young MP was. Mukherjee was later introduced to Indira Gandhi by CPI leader Bhupesh Gupta. After that, Pranab became quite close to Mrs Gandhi and never looked back.

In 1973, he joined the Cabinet as Union Deputy Minister for Industrial Development. He rose through a series of Cabinet posts to become the Finance Minister of India from 1982 to 1984.

He went on to become a close confidant of Indira Gandhi and became almost indispensable to her. The following incident narrated by Pranab clearly indicates this.

With a childish grin, Mukherjee would say how 'Indira Gandhi' repeatedly asked him not to contest the 1980 Lok

Sabha poll. But he, keen to shed the perception of being a 'rootless wonder', fought and lost.

In the evening a call came from Delhi at his Kolkata residence. At the other end, there was a furious Indira Gandhi. "Everyone knew that you will lose. Even Geeta (Mukherjee's wife's pet name) knew it. But still you went ahead and created trouble for me," she hung up without even allowing him to reply. Two days later, another call came. This time, Sanjay Gandhi spoke: "Mummy is very angry with you, but she also said, 'there can't be any cabinet without Pranab'. Take a flight for Delhi tomorrow".

He was not included in Rajiv Gandhi's Cabinet after Lok Sabha election, held subsequent to Indira Gandhi's brutal assassination in 1984. He was pushed out of the Congress party for a brief period, and during this period he formed his own political party Rashtriya Samajwadi Congress, but later merged it with Congress party in 1989, after a settlement with Rajiv Gandhi. His political career revived when PV Narasimha Rao chose to appoint him as Deputy Chairman of the Planning Commission (1991-1996) and subsequently as External Affairs Minister for the first time from 1995 to 1996, in his cabinet.

Pranab was the President of the West Bengal state unit of Congress since 1985, but resigned in July 2010 due to heavy work-load and was succeeded by Manas Bhunia. In 2004, when the Congress formed a coalition government at the Centre (United Progressive Alliance- UPA 1), the new Congress Prime Minister Manmohan Singh was only a Member of Rajya Sabha. So Pranab Mukherjee was made Leader of the House in the Lok Sabha, as he had won the Lok Sabha elections for the first time from Jangipur Lok Sabha constituency.

Pranab Da played crucial role in steering the Cabinet prior to the Lok Sabha elections in 2009, when the Prime Minister Dr Manmohan Singh underwent a by-pass surgery, by taking additional charges as chairman of the Cabinet Committee on Political Affairs and Union Minister in Finance Ministry, despite already being Union Minister of External Affairs.

Pranab Mukherjee in his successful and eventful political career played many crucial roles at the international level also.

Other Roles

- Pranab Mukherjee played a central role in the implementation of the Indo-US civil nuclear agreement. Mukherjee and US Secretary of State Condoleezza Rice signed the Section 123 Agreement on October 10, 2008.
- He has been a member of the Board of Governors of the International Monetary Fund, of the World Bank, of the Asian Development Bank, and of the African Development Bank.
- In 1984, he chaired the Group of 24 attached to the IMF and World Bank.
- Between May and November 1995, he presided over the SAARC Council of Ministers Conference.
- Appointed by Prime Minister Manmohan Singh to ease issues over the anti-corruption campaign initiated by Anna Hazare, on August 23, 2011, the eighth day of Anna Hazare's fast.

Political Party Role

Mukherjee was very well-respected within the party social circles. Other media accounts describe him as having a reputation as a number-crunching politician, with a phenomenal memory and an unerring survival instinct.

After Sonia Gandhi reluctantly agreed to join politics, Mukherjee was one of her key mentors, guiding her through difficult situations with examples of how her mother-in-law, Indira Gandhi would have done things. Mukherjee's unfailing loyalty and competence have led to his closeness to Sonia Gandhi and Manmohan Singh, and helped him gain the position of Minister of Defence, when the party came to power in 2004.

Negotiation Skills

Pranab talents as a consummate negotiator were on display during the negotiations for the Patent's Amendment Bill in early 2005. The Congress was committed to passing an Intellectual Property (IP) Bill, but their allies in the United Progressive Alliance-1, the Left Front, had a long tradition of opposing some of the monopoly aspects of intellectual property. Pranab Mukherjee, as Defence Minister, was not formally involved but was roped in for his negotiation skills. He drew on many old alliances including the CPI-M leader Jyoti Basu, and formed new intermediary positions, which included product patent. Then he had to convince his own colleagues including commerce minister Kamal Nath, at one point saying: "An imperfect legislation is better than no legislation". Finally the Bill was approved on March 23, 2005.

Pranab Da has subsequently proved to be a deft negotiator for the UPA government, dealing both with coalition partners and opposition, in steering the Parliament through numerous deadlocks.

His foresight and analytical mind was greatly respected by Sonia Gandhi even in political affairs.

A meeting of the Congress brass called after the 2002 assembly election of Jammu & Kashmir, perhaps marked a new level of trust between Sonia Gandhi and Mukherjee. In the meeting, all other leaders except Mukherjee and Arjun Singh reportedly favoured that Congress should take the chief minister's chair first, in the coalition government with the People's Democratic Party (PDP). Mukherjee strongly argued why the local party should be given the Chief Minister's post first in the rotation. Towards the end of the meeting, Sonia Gandhi took a final opinion of all leaders and told Mukherjee, "You are miserably defeated".

Mukherjee replied, "I know I am defeated. But I also know I am right".

Three days later, Sonia Gandhi called PDP's Mufti Muhammad Sayeed and his daughter Mehbooba and asked them to take the chief minister's post.

In another incidence, when there was a need to drop Adarsh-tainted Ashok Chavan as Maharashtra Chief Minister in 2010, Mrs Gandhi sent Mukherjee along with AK Antony (the party in-charge for Maharashtra). The two leaders returned to the capital from Mumbai around 3 am. Within a few minutes, Mukherjee's cell phone rang and to his utter disbelief, it was Sonia Gandhi on the line. "How can I go to sleep when you two are still awake and working?" Mrs Gandhi quipped and asked them to come over to 10 Janpath, for a meeting.

Commerce Minister

Mukherjee has thrice served as Commerce Minister of India. His first stints were in the Indira Gandhi government from 1980–82 and again in 1984. His third stint in the 1990s saw him contribute significantly to the negotiations leading to the establishment of the World Trade Organisation.

Defence Minister

Manmohan Singh appointed Mukherjee as the Minister of Defence of India when the Congress came to power in 2004. Mukherjee held the post till 2006. He expanded co-operation with the United States during his tenure. Wikileaks cables release and noted how "United States is full of praise for the 'uniformed leadership' of Indian armed forces, especially Navy, as well as ministers like Mukherjee". Mukherjee in June 2005 had inked the 10-year Indo-US Defence Framework deal.

Despite increasing co-operation with the United States, Mukherjee maintained that Russia will remain India's 'topmost' defence partner. He asserted that "Russia has been and will remain India's largest defence partner in the years to come" while inaugurating the 5th session of the Indo-Russian Inter-Governmental Commission on Military

Technical Cooperation (IRIGC-MTC) in Moscow in 2005.

Russia held the first joint anti-terror war games with India in Rajasthan in October 2005, during which Mukherjee and Russian Defence Minister Sergei Ivanov narrowly escaped injury after a heavy mortar landed several metres from their platform. The Russian ministry subsequently declared its hopes to follow up joint military exercises in India with further joint exercises on Russian territory.

Foreign Minister

Pranab Mukherjee was appointed as foreign minister by the then prime minister PV Narasimha Rao in 1995. Under his leadership, India was made "Full Dialogue Partner" of ASEAN as part of the Look East foreign policy initiated by Narasimha Rao. Mukherjee left the position in 1996.

In 2004, he was appointed Defence Minister by Manmohan Singh Government and again in 2006, he was shifted from Defence Ministry to the External Affairs Ministry replacing AK Antony former Chief Minister of Kerala.

When Pranab Mukherjee was shifted to External Affairs Ministry from Defence Ministry, he called up his successor AK Antony to say, "Antony I am handing over to you, all my sleepless nights".

Mukherjee was briefly considered for the post of the largely ceremonial Indian presidency. But his name was subsequently dropped after his contribution in the Union Cabinet was considered practically indispensable. Among Mukherjee's current legacy as External Affairs minister was the successful signing of the US-India Civil Nuclear Agreement with the US government, and then with the Nuclear Suppliers Group, allowing India to participate in civilian nuclear trade, in spite of not having signed the Nuclear Non-Proliferation Treaty. He visited America in 2008 as External Affairs Minister and met the then President George W Bush for the Indo-US civil nuclear agreement, which led to the eventual signing of this path breaking treaty, after protracted negotiations, wherein Pranab Da played a stellar role.

Finance Minister

Pranab Mukherjee's first stint as the Finance Minister of India was during the Indira Gandhi government in 1982. He presented his first annual budget in 1982-83. Manmohan Singh was serving as Governor of the Reserve Bank of India, during Pranab's term as Finance Minister.

Though, he never studied economics, yet he proved his credential as a successful finance minister. He was selected as one of the best five finance ministers of the world in 1984 by a New York journal, *Euro Money*. He also acted as Economic Advisory Cell chairman of All India Congress Committee from 1987 to 1989.

In the second government of Manmohan Singh (UPA II), he again became the Finance Minister, a job he had held earlier in the 1980s.

De Facto PM

Many people who know Mukherjee, including Somnath Chatterjee, a former Speaker of the Lok Sabha, believe that he has been the de facto Prime Minister in the two UPA governments. There's one very compelling reason to believe so.

Since 2004, a strange institution called 'Empowered Group of Ministers' (EGoM), has sprung up. It's a small group of '*mantris*,' relevant to a particular issue, who get into a huddle to take important policy decisions, if the cabinet, the highest policy-making body in the country, can't take a call.

These EGoMs have tackled issues as diverse as the pricing of natural gas, and allocation of radio spectrum. At one point Mukherjee was heading 13 out of the 14 EGoMs. Any decision taken by the EGoM is final: it doesn't need the cabinets' or the prime minister's approval.

"There's a reason why he heads them," says a senior Congress politician. "The government knows if the matter goes to the EGoM, Mukherjee will not let it go without finding a solution".

Mukherjee's activism doesn't end with policy wrangles. He's the chief troubleshooter when ally like Mamata Banerjee throws one of her tantrums. He was the man who brought Anna Hazare to discussion table after efforts by colleagues like Palaniappan Chidambaram and Kapil Sibal backfired.

After Mamata Banerjee shook up the UPA II regime by demanding the scalp of her party colleague and railway minister Dinesh Trivedi for hiking the railway fares in the 2012 Rail Budget, it was Mukherjee who called her, and got her to hold her horses, till the budget session break for recess, before doing anything.

More on Pranab Babu, as Told by Pradyut Guha

Pradyut Guha, Pranab Mukherjee's personal assistant shared the known and unknown facts about 'the man of the moment', in his own words.

Guha says, "The journey of Pranab Mukherjee from 13, Talkatora Road to Rashtrapati Bhavan to become the 13th President of India has been steady and eventful. Destiny's man who did not become Prime Minister (PM), but ran the country as a de facto PM is a 'normal', down to earth human being with normal Indian traits, likes and dislikes. After he was nominated as the presidential candidate of the Congress, hundreds of people called on him to express their pleasure. A man, even though was never considered to be a mass leader, got the adulation of the masses during the last few weeks of campaigning".

Pradyut Guha was a youth leader in Kolkata when he first met Pranab Da in 1972. Guha has been involved in social and political activities since the last three decades.

Pradyut Guha says modestly, "I am a political colleague of Pranab Da". In the last eight years he has worked with Pranab Da in three ministries - defence, external affairs and finance.

When Pranab Da was Finance Minister, Guha's room was located on one side of his office and on the other side was Omita Paul's, another confidante of Pranab Da.

In an interview, Guha regrets that Pranab Babu could not become PM but was happy to see him shift to the majestic Rashtrapati Bhavan on Raisina Hills.

Guha's First Encounter

Guha elaborates, "In 1977, when Indira Gandhi lost the Election after the unforgettable episodes of Emergency, Pranab Mukherjee became the first Congressman to back her and started canvassing in her favour".

Guha continues, "Pranab Babu toured the country to gather Congress workers and convince them, not to desert Indira Gandhi or the Congress, in view of the defeat. In Kolkata, a Congress workers meeting was convened at the Nizam's Palace. At that time Siddhartha Shankar Ray, Ashok Sen and Priya Ranjan Dasmunshi and many others had left the party. I was at the meeting. Sentimental attachment left us confused, when we saw leaders like Ray and Dasmunshi leaving the party. But when Pranab Da, in his inimitable way, voiced the real political picture and explained Indira Gandhi and Sanjay Gandhi's role in it, things got clear. After that meeting we were convinced, not to desert the Congress party".

"In him I saw my leader. A front-ranking leader of India," Guha said with pride. "Pranab Mukherjee has convinced generations of Congress workers to stay true to their party. Despite the struggle for three years after emergency, I was so impressed with his speech at the meeting, that I banished all thoughts of leaving him or the party ever", he said.

The Nationalist

In Mamata Didi's words, "Pranab Da always keeps the national angle in focus. He is not only for his home state Bengal but he is a national leader, in fact a global leader".

"The Congress is a 127-year-old party. Its district and block level leaders should also have the national angle in mind. Having grown up in a politically oriented family, he totally understands the nitty gritties of grass-root politics of the Congress party. Added to that his humble beginnings, helps him to empathize and understand people, especially Congress workers with whom he has been associated right from the district level. But he remains an Indian first. It is not in his nature to favour a particular village, district or state", confirmed Pradyut Guha.

"Even though he has held many portfolios his focus has always been in the interest of the nation. He is a true nationalist, a true Indian always working towards a better and prosperous India. Pranab babu's friendly nature is known to all. He behaves like an elder brother to me, while to some he is the proverbial uncle," said Guha.

"Pranab Da has been the most approachable 'father figure' to the people in Congress, in times of need. Not only was he considered a 'problem solver' in political affairs, even grass-root workers came to him when confronted with problems of finance, admissions in schools and colleges or for medical expenses. Pranab Da's humane side is extraordinary and fantastic. In the last 42 years, I have worked with many leaders but Pranab Da is more than a politician, he is a perfect gentleman; easily comparable to Rajiv Gandhi, who was a gentleman first and then a politician. Pranab Da's strength lies in his clarity of thought and his decision-making skills but the magic touch lies in, how well he gift wraps what has to be conveyed. In clear, soft, respectful but a firm tone," said Pradyut.

Pradyut Guha continued, "Pranab Mukherjee is a man of great intellectual abilities, but he is not a mass leader. This was a generalised statement made quite often by people. I too believed it, till 1990. The Jangipur election in 2004 dispelled all doubts. Congress had been unsuccessful in winning from this constituency for quite a while. But Pranab Da won from here by a margin of 38,000 votes".

His Temper

Guha said he got an irritated response when he had asked him once, "Dada lots of people say you are not a mass leader".

Raising his eyebrows, he looked agitated and said, "You don't know how many people I have helped, the connections I have with innumerable people. It's just that I don't believe in publicity".

"Well that is really true. He meets many people away from the camera, away from public gaze. Yes, at times he loses his temper too quickly but, he controls it and calms down within minutes. But despite the anger, he still thinks in a sane manner and does not lose focus in making a sound judgment", explains Pradyut Guha.

"After the 2004 elections, he asked me to join his office, i.e., the Ministry of Defence in South Block. One day Congress MLA Moin-ul-Haq from Farakka constituency was called by the police at midnight. He was thrashed in the police station and put in the lock-up. When I came to know about it in the morning, I was very angry. I used to look after his constituency. I called up the local police officer on duty and the police confirmed his arrest", Guha recalls.

Guha telephoned the senior Superintendent of Police to inform him about what had happened. The Superintendent of Police saw to it that the junior police officer, who had arrested Mr Haq, was transferred out of station immediately.

Pradyut Guha then said, "I felt very proud. I thought I had taken good care of the party leader. While sitting in his car, I narrated the incident to Pranab Da. To my utter surprise he was livid, he seemed to have a temper meltdown and yelled, "This is not the Youth Congress. This is the ministry of defence. You are not president of the Youth Congress. You are private secretary of Pranab Mukherjee".

"I was shocked. I told Dada I had been helping people since the days when I was president of the Youth Congress". said Guha.

Pranab Da said angrily, "I told you this is not the Youth Congress. This is the Government of India! You are in government. Before calling a government officer you must inquire. The policeman is a government servant too. You should have asked what the fault of the MLA was. Why was he arrested? Was he drunk? Did he flout any law? Was he driving on the wrong side of the road?"

Guha recalls, "I had not got any information about the arrest of the MLA, before calling the police officer. Pranab Da's anger was justified, so I promptly apologised and from then onwards taking his advice seriously I amended my working style".

Regret

Pradyut Guha also said "Pranab Mukherjee will never display any disappointment, but, I believe, he has been deprived. Much earlier, he should have got the number one chair in the government. He should have become prime minister of India. He is fit for any portfolio in the government, because his uptake on political matters is extremely sharp. He effortlessly takes in information provided to him. In 2004, when he became defence minister, he went to the office, took a cup of tea and without much fanfare called the defence secretary, to get the defence scenario in its true perspective. Now that he is the President, he is sensitive and well-experienced to understand the duties and responsibilities, his job demands".

According to Pradyut Guha words "The only time Pranab Da overreacted, he has regretted. After Indira Gandhi's assassination, he fell out with Rajiv Gandhi and floated Rashtriya Samajwadi Congress. He said it was a mistake to leave Congress and form a new party. In fact, he told me, he should have waited to talk it out with Rajiv Gandhi. Of course all that is well behind him now".

Detailed Recap (1969-2012)

Pranab Mukherjee assumed office as the 13th President of India on July 25, 2012, crowning a political career of over five decades of exemplary service to the nation in Government as well as Parliament.

An avid traveller, there are few parts of India and few countries in the world he has not visited in his illustrious and long public career.

Administrative Career

Deputy Minister, Industrial Development: February 1973 to January 1974.

Deputy Minister, Shipping and Transport: January 1974 to October 1974

Minister of State for Finance: October 1974 to December 1975

Minister of State for Revenue and Banking (Independent Charge): December 1975 to March 1977

Cabinet Minister of Commerce and Steel and Mines: January 1980 to January 1982

Cabinet Minister of Finance: January 1982 to December 1984

Additional charge of the Ministry of Commerce and Supply: September to December 31, 1984

Deputy Chairman, Planning Commission: June 1991 to May 1996

Cabinet Minister of Commerce: January 1993 to February 1995

Cabinet Minister of External Affairs: February 1995 to May 1996

Cabinet Minister of Defence: May 2004 to 24 October 2006

Cabinet Minister of External Affairs: October 2006 to May 2009

Cabinet Minister of Finance: 24 January 2009 to 26 June 2012

Parliamentary Career

Elected to Rajya Sabha: 1969, 1975, 1981, 1993, 1999

Elected to Lok Sabha: 2004, 2009, upto July 2012

Deputy Leader of the Congress Party in the Rajya Sabha: 1978-80

Chief Whip of Congress Party in the Rajya Sabha: 1996-2004

Leader of House in the Rajya Sabha: 1980-85

Member, Business Advisory Committee, Committee on Privileges and Committee on Rules

Member, Consultative Committee on External Affairs: 1996-99

Chairman, Parliament Standing Committee on Science and Technology, Environment and Forests: 1997

Chairman, Parliament Standing Committee on Home Affairs : June 1998 to May 2004

Leader of the Lok Sabha: June 2004 to June 2012

Career in the Congress Party

Member, Congress Working Committee: January 27, 1978 to January 18, 1986, August 10, 1997 till June 25, 2012

President, West Bengal Pradesh Congress Committee: 1985, August 2000 to June, 2010

Member, Central Parliamentary Board, All India Congress Committee (AICC): 1978 to 1986

Treasurer of the AICC: 1978 to 1979

Treasurer of the Congress (I) Party in Parliament: 1978 to 1979

Chairman, Economic Advisory Cell, AICC: 1987 to 1989

Chairman, Campaign Committee of the AICC for conducting National Elections to Parliament: 1984, 1991, 1996. 1998, 1999

Chairman, Central Election Coordination Committee of the

AICC: June 28, 1999 onwards

Member, Central Election Committee, AICC: December 12, 2001 to 25 June, 2012

Resigned from the Congress Party prior to contesting to the office of President of India: 25 June, 2012

Membership in International Organizations

Board of Governors of the International Monetary Fund (IMF): 1982 to 1985, 2009 - 2012

Board of Governors, World Bank: 1982 to 1985, 2009 to 2012

Board of Governors, Asian Development Bank (ADB): 1982 to 1985, 2009 to 2012

Board of Governors, African Development Bank: 1982 to 1985, 2009 to 2012

Chairman, Group of 24 nations in IMF and World Bank: 1984, 2011-12

Chairman, South Asian Association for Regional Cooperation (SAARC), Council of Ministers Conference: May 1995, November 1995, April 2007

Leadership of Indian delegations abroad

Colombo Plan Finance Ministers' Conference, Singapore and Colombo: 1975, 1976

The Commonwealth Finance Ministers' Conferences: 1982, 1983, 1984

The Annual Meetings of the World Bank and IMF: 1982, 1983, 1984, 2009, 2010, 2011, 2012

Annual Meetings of the ADB: 1982, 1983, 1984, 2010, 2011, 2012

Ministerial Conference of WTO at Marrakesh: 1994

The United Nations General Assembly: 1994, 1995, 2005, 2006

The Social Summit at Copenhagen: 1995

The 40th Anniversary of the Afro-Asian Conference at Bandung: 1995

The Conference of Commonwealth Heads of Government (CHOGM), Auckland: 1995

The Non-Aligned Foreign Minister's Conference, Cartagena: 1995

Social and Cultural Activities

President of the Nikhil Bharat Banga Sahitya Sammelan: 1995 to 2001, 2004 to June 2012

Chairman, Planning Board, Asiatic Society, Kolkata: 1984 to 1986, 1992 to 1996, 2004-2012

Trustee, Bangiya Sahitya Parishad: 1984 to 1990

Trustee Bidhan Memorial Trust, Kolkata: 1998 to June 2012

Books Authored

Mid-term Poll (1969)

Beyond Survival: Emerging Dimensions of Indian Economy: 1984

Off the Track: 1987

Saga of Struggle and Sacrifice: 1992

Challenges before the Nation (on Indian National Congress): 1992

Jatiya Congress-er Katha (In Bengali)

Dada's famous quotes

Pranab Babu can also display an uncanny sense of humour and has the ability to take a joke on himself. There are several jokes about his thick Bengali-accented English. A famous one is that he once said in context of disproportionate assets cases against the AIADMK chief, "Joylolitha cannot be *shaved* (Jayalalitha cannot be saved)". But the short man never felt ashamed about these shortcomings. In fact, he once told one of his US-educated cabinet colleague, "I studied at my village school and then at a local college. I didn't receive foreign education like you. But yes, I know what the real India is, which perhaps you don't know".

Some of the other remarkable quotes attributed to Pranab are:

- To the then US Defence Secretary Donald Rumsfeld during a bilateral meeting:-

  "You say that you are helping Pakistan to fight terror. Tell me, which terror camp will be attacked by the F16s you plan to supply to Pakistan".

- To BJP leader Ram Jethmalani in the Rajya Sabha during a debate:-

  "Infiltrators don't stand in queue at the LoC and ask, please come and count our number. There is no fool-proof method of knowing the number of terrorists who enter India every year".

- To Pakistan foreign minister after 26/11, Mumbai attacks:-

  "Even these non-state actors don't come from heaven. They operate from your soil".

- To former finance minister Yashwant Sinha who said in budget debate that the tax relief is insufficient even to buy a bottle of whiskey!

  "My suggestion is, you stop drinking whiskey. It is not good for health".

Chapter - IV

Left the Congress Party

Rajiv and Pranab were campaigning in West Bengal when Indira Gandhi was gunned down mercilessly by her trusted security guards in New Delhi in 1984. Arguably that was the most shocking incident in the annals of the Indian political history. Aftermath of the incident was another unforgettable yet macabre episode happened in the form of anti-Sikh riots which was more tragic when the innocents Sikhs were either killed or burnt alive by angry people.

So, both Rajiv and Pranab were flown back to New Delhi together on a special flight. There are several versions of what transpired between them during the flight. Apparently, Rajiv asked Pranab who should be the interim Prime Minister at this crucial juncture. Playing with a straight bat he informed Rajiv that the senior most ministers became caretaker PM after Jawaharlal Nehru's and Lal Bahadur Shastri's death. Left unsaid, was that Pranab was Indira's senior most minister in the cabinet then.

Pranab's straight forward reply became an albatross around his neck. There are reports that after the fateful conversation, Pranab had retreated to the rear of the aircraft, where he wept inconsolably for his mentor Indira Ji's sudden and heartless killing. Subsequently, he was accused of sitting at a distance from Rajiv and plotting.

Pranab soon detected ominous signs. First, there were insinuations that he had prime ministerial ambitions. Then, Rajiv's drum-beaters in the media announced that Pranab had forcefully staked his claim to the throne. Retribution for the 'crime' was swift. There was no place for Pranab in Rajiv's new cabinet after the landslide victory on the sympathy wave of her mother Indira Gandhi. Pranab was branded not only ambitious and scheming, but corrupt and shady also; Pranab turned into a *persona non grata* virtually overnight. There were orchestrated demands to sack him. And soon after, Rajiv expelled him from the Congress.

There were reports of Pranab's passport being impounded and his residences in Delhi and Kolkata being raided. Pushed to the wall, Pranab floated the Rashtriya Samajwadi Congress Party, which contested the 1987 assembly polls in Bengal but didn't win a single seat. Pranab's misery piled up, he was not re-elected to the Rajya Sabha when his term expired in 1987; he ceased to be an MP after 17 long years. Clearly, Rajiv's objective was to humiliate and marginalise Pranab, turning 1985-88 into the most depressing chapters of his political career.

Victim of an Intrigue

Swapan Ghosh, a Congress worker close to Pranab for thirty years, says that Rajiv-Pranab relations hit such a low, that Pranab's letter to Rajiv informing him about his father Kamada Kinkar Mukherjee's death was not replied to. Pranab waited for a condolence message but in vain. When Pranab met Rajiv much later, Rajiv said he never got the letter. Swapan's surmise is that Pranab's letter was intercepted by the coterie surrounding Rajiv in those days and destroyed, lest it evoked Rajiv's sympathy and paved the way for Pranab's return.

But few party men believe Pranab is far too loyal and steeped in Congress culture to have posed a threat to Rajiv or Sonia. "Let's call it a monumental misunderstanding," they said. Pranab became a victim of a 'palace intrigue.' Many new faces had infiltrated Rajiv's inner circle after Indira's demise. Their machinations—and Rajiv's tendency to believe them— totally knocked Pranab out of orbit. So it took Rajiv, who probably realised his mistake, a while to pull Pranab back to where he belonged.

Both Rajiv and Pranab bore the brunt of slanderous campaigns and their victimisation is a fit subject for research by political analysts. But the irony is inescapable; Rajiv imperiously expelled Pranab from the Congress—only to come under a much bigger cloud himself, soon after. The Bofors scandal maligned and destroyed Rajiv's reputation and cost the Congress the 1989 elections. He was brutally killed while campaigning in 1991 for the Lok Sabha elections. The Delhi High Court cleared Rajiv of bribery charges many years later as late as 2004, prompting Sonia's remark, that her husband always said that one day, his innocence would be proved as he was deliberately implicated in this row.

Even VP Singh, who engineered his downfall in the first place, long after his tragic death admitted that, perhaps Rajiv was unfairly targeted. In contrast, Pranab, a devout and ardent believer in divine justice, is now about to cap, what must now count, as the mother of all comebacks.

Abhijit Mukherjee, Pranab's 52-year-old son, who left SAIL last year to become a Congress MLA in West Bengal and is now elected as the Member of Parliament after winning the Pranab's Jangipur Parliamentary seat, says, "My father first stepped into the Rajya Sabha the day Neil Armstrong stepped on the moon in July 1969. In 1973, he became a Union Minister, and was re-elected in 1975 and 1981. Indira Gandhi, who had a soft corner for the Bengali Babu, made Pranab the Finance Minister in 1982. Life was a bed of roses for Pranab as he became the close confidant of Indiraji. Indira frequently picked his brain, even as India's rich and powerful paid obeisance to her. But his world suddenly turned upside down on October 31, 1984, when Indira Gandhi was brutally gunned down" by her security guards.

Exile Was Uncalled For

It was really a pity that an innocent man like Pranab was unnecessarily hounded and exiled. If anyone wrecked Rajiv, it was VP Singh, Amitabh Bachchan and Arun Nehru. For VP Singh, loyalty was a means to give a further boost his own career. The moment he got an opportunity, he stabbed Rajiv in the back and felled him riding on the crest of Bofors gun deal controversy. Rajiv could never recover from that severe blow, dealt by his own so-called loyalist. Similarly, Amitabh's act of vacating the Allahabad seat to clear the deck for VP Singh's victory in the bye election helped the opposition to regroup and attack Rajiv. This sent a clear message that Rajiv could be humbled despite his 415 Lok Sabha seats. According to Priyanka Gandhi's assessment, Arun Nehru was a saboteur and the enemy within. There is no dearth of analysts who believe that the Bofors scandal wouldn't have extracted such a big toll, if Rajiv had reposed his faith in politicians of the Indira School like Pranab Mukherjee, instead of side tracking them, for no substantial reason.

Rehabilitated

According to his son Abhijit -- Pranab's friends, like GK Moopanar, whose son GK Vasan is now the minister for shipping, played an important role in the rapprochement between Pranab and Rajiv. One fine morning Pranab was given charge of the AICC media cell. Then, he was made AICC spokesman. Pranab was rehabilitated, but couldn't regain his former glory during Rajiv's lifetime. He had to wait until PV Narasimha Rao appointed him Deputy Chairman of the Planning Commission. In 1993, he re-entered the Rajya Sabha and was quickly re-inducted into the cabinet as Foreign Minister.

PV Narasimha Rao also shielded him against occasional efforts of Mukherjee's detractors within the Congress to retire him.

Once a group of senior Congressmen explained at length why Pranab Mukherjee should be made the Governor of Uttar Pradesh, a politically crucial state for the Congress. Rao heard them with his trademark patience, and then replied: "Already 90 per cent of our voters have gone to Samajwadi Party (SP) and other parties. If Pranab becomes UP Governor, his Hindi speaking skills will force the rest of the 10 per cent to run away as well".

Loyal he always was, but Pranab Da has proved he is a fighter to the core. The way he made his comeback and stood tall, as also made himself, an indispensable figure in the party, bears testimony to his indomitable spirit.

The Congress President Sonia Gandhi, inadvertently might have righted a wrong, by nominating Pranab Mukherjee for the presidency of the Republic, in the twilight of his political life, just because her late husband Rajiv Gandhi had unfairly shown door to Pranab, from the Congress party.

Unwavering Loyalty

The 77-year-old leader from Bengal is made from sterner stuff. He eventually crawled out of the moribund phase, and painstakingly proved his loyalty many times, for over two decades, belying Rajiv's doubts in the bargain. By proving his loyalty to the party, he managed to silence his detractors to a great extent and regained the confidence of the person who was at the helm of affairs. And, the late Prime Minister Rajiv's widow was left with no choice but to acknowledge Pranab's unwavering loyalty to the Gandhi family, and his life-long services to the party, by nominating him for the country's highest constitutional post for the next five years.

In a sense, Sonia is a far more astute a politician than Rajiv. Her astuteness is actually what allowed Pranab to regain his deserving niche in the hierarchy. She has the uncanny knack of choosing horses for courses. So she gave Pranab, the task of eliminating Sitaram Kesri, and instructed Jitendra Prasada to provide operational support. The plot to get rid of Sitaram, who wanted to remain Congress president until his death, was formulated in Pranab's house, culminating in the March 14, 1998, reshuffle. Sonia gleefully replaced Sitaram, as party president; a post she still holds, making her the longest serving president in Congress history. At the time of NCP leaders Sharad Pawar, Tariq Anwar and PA Sangma's revolting due to Sonia Gandhi's Italian roots, Pranab dutifully led the rearguard action, against the mutineers at the behest of the Congress President. People in the know, also acknowledges that it was Pranab, who drafted Sonia's letters during that critical period. His English is not good in the English-speaking world, but his insight into Indian politics certainly is the best.

Chapter - V

As a Foreign Minister

Evolutionary not Revolutionary

Pranab Mukherjee has been India's Minister for External Affairs, twice. He led the country's foreign policy at a critical time when India was emerging as a force to reckon with on the world stage, despite surrounded by increasingly unstable and hostile neighbours.

Pranab Mukherjee became the Foreign Minister for the first time, in 1995-96 in PV Narasimha Rao's Government and again appointed as the External Affairs Minister of India, in 2006-09 in UPA-1 Government, led by Dr Manmohan Singh.

Among Mukherjee's current legacy was the successful signing of the US-India Civil Nuclear Agreement with the US government and then with the Nuclear Suppliers Group, allowing India to participate in civil nuclear trade in spite of not having signed the Nuclear Non-Proliferation Treaty.

Pranab Mukherjee faced quite some challenges, on the Gandhian values dictating India's foreign policy. As External Affairs Minister Pranab Mukherjee believed, Indian foreign policy owes a great deal to Mahatma Gandhi's philosophy of peace and non-violence. According to Mukherjee, India's foreign policy is based on *Panchsheel* propounded by Pandit Nehru, which was itself drawn from the Gandhian philosophy of peace and non-violence; the path of truth and passive resistance espoused by Mahatma Gandhi.

The five principles of *Panchsheel* are:

- Respect for each other's territorial integrity
- Non-aggression
- Non-interference in each other's internal affairs
- Equality
- Peaceful coexistence

These principles have now become accepted norms of bilateral relations between neighbouring nations and have been recognised throughout the world. He generously praised Gandhi for making *satyagraha* the "soul" of his politics and public life.

Underlining the relevance of Gandhi in the 21st century beset by terrorism and many violent conflicts in the world, Pranab said, "Gandhi put the human being at the centre of all planning and future development".

A Roadmap for a Decade Ahead: Major Role in Economic Renaissance

Mukherjee shares a few thoughts on the roadmap for India's foreign policy in the years ahead:

"It is a product of history, geopolitical setting and the needs and aspirations of its people as distilled by its democratic institutions". This policy is inspired by the vision of our founding fathers, in particular Pandit Nehru, and is nourished by a tradition of continuity and consensus.

India's Foreign Policy is poised to play a major role in economic renaissance. There is a range of foreign policy instruments available today to advance our economic interests - traditional commercial work, negotiation of preferential or free trading areas, active participation in multilateral forums etc.

The government needs to creatively add to this toolbox, and in fact retune mindsets so that our entire approach to a bilateral relationship is premised primarily on that relationship's contribution to our economic well-being. What is needed, to list only a few, include a significant upgrading of our economic relationship with South East Asia, East Asia, Latin America and Africa, building new investment driven partnerships with the US and EU and nurturing a web of cooperative energy security networks in Asia and with new suppliers in West Africa, Central Asia and Latin America.

Traditionally threats to India's security have largely come overland from the North and the West and from the waters in the South and the West. In future the importance of the East in the country's security calculus is slated to rise. Maritime security, Weapons of Mass Destruction (WMD) proliferation, energy security and terrorism are important and emerging issues with a bearing on the security of the region. The emphasis should be to promote an environment of peace and security in the region and beyond, which indeed is a pre-requisite for development.

Relations with Neighbours

The other major theme for Indian Foreign Policy a decade hence, has to be a significantly different set of relationships in the neighbourhood. A major power has hardly ever emerged, or sustained itself, on the international scene from amidst a conflict-ridden and impoverished neighbourhood. The street, on which India has to build a future home, should reflect our values and our aspirations, in particular our desire for a peaceful and prosperous future. India, as the largest country in South Asia with land and sea borders with all its neighbours in the South Asian Association for Regional Cooperation (SAARC), and indeed as the eldest 'sister' in South Asia, has to assume greater responsibility for the region's challenges.

India's neighbours can and should share in our drive for prosperity. Bhutan, for example, has significantly raised its per capita income as a result of its energy exports to India. Sri Lanka has drawn full value from its importance to the logistics of Indian trade. Both Maldives and Sri Lanka are benefiting from Indian tourism. So too is Mauritius, which also serves as an investment route into India. Citizens of Nepal have long sought employment opportunities in India, a trend that will only become stronger. More recently, China has discovered the advantages of trading with India, and our bilateral trade is growing at an astonishing 60 per cent plus per annum. With Thailand, India has concluded an FTA and with Myanmar, we are exploring new opportunities in energy and infrastructure. Afghanistan has benefited from the participation of Indian companies in its reconstruction and economic revival.

Indo-Pak Relations

The coming decade is crucial for India-Pakistan relations, which even today are at the crossroads. It is not easy to change borders, but the country can surely make efforts to strengthen bilateral relationship. Initiatives that promote people-to-people relations have resulted in the deep yearning amongst ordinary people, for peace and normalcy. Sustaining and expanding this process would be one of the important challenges of India's foreign policy. But this can happen only when diplomacy is allowed to function without interruption. If, on the other hand, terrorism is perceived and practised as an instrument of statecraft, then the most imaginative diplomacy will be founded on lack of domestic support.

Relations with Major Powers

India's relations with the major powers - United States, European Union, Russia, China and Japan as well as the emerging powers of Latin America and Africa have undergone a major makeover in the past decade and a half. The bandwidth of engagement with these powers is wider than ever. India's Foreign Policy would need to actively promote the building of a qualitatively different relationship, with the major powers in the decade ahead thus contributing positively to our political, economic, and security objectives.

The exponential and qualitative change in India-US relations has rightly attracted global attention. The India-US civil nuclear agreement symbolizes not only a maturing of bilateral relations but also a clear recognition of the responsible record of India, as a state possessing advanced nuclear technologies. India's cooperation on matters impinging on regional and international security is a reflection and recognition of its capabilities and its role in fostering peace and security. As India grows and integrates with the global economy, there is bound to be more demand for US goods, technology and services and at the same time greater penetration of the vast US market by Indian companies. There is another evolving significant factor, of complementarities in human resources as people to people exchanges take place. All these have the potential to unleash a much broader and deeper strategic engagement between the two countries.

India's strategic partnership with Russia has had to weather the difficulties thrown up after the disintegration of the Soviet Union. Developments in the post-Cold War period have imposed different sets of constraints but have also offered newer options for both India and Russia. For India, Russia is a partner in fight against global terrorism, an ally in the field of civil nuclear, space and defence technologies and a key player in the quest for energy sufficiency.

India and Europe share values of democracy, pluralism, human rights and respect for rule of law with similar institutions such as a free press and an independent judiciary. India is now one of European Union's (EU's) six strategic partners and the EU remains India's largest export destination and one of the largest sources of foreign investment into India. India's strategic partnership is based on mutual interest and the great potential both sides see for enhanced cooperation, including in tackling global problems such as terrorism and environmental degradation.

India's 'Look East' policy was more than an economic imperative. It was a significant shift in India's vision of the world and her place in the emerging post-Cold War global scenario. In the years to come it will be our endeavour to strengthen political, physical and economic connectivity between India and East Asia and broaden the underpinnings of our quest for peace and prosperity.

The India-China relationship is bound to be one of the most important bilateral relationships in the coming decade simply by the sheer weight of demographic and economic numbers. How India manages its relationship will have a tremendous impact on peace and stability in the regional and increasingly the global context. India-China relations have traditionally been viewed through the prism of 'balance of power' or 'conflict of interests' with Asia as the theatre of competition. This theory has become outdated in today's interconnected and interdependent world. It is increasingly recognised that there is enough space and opportunity for both to grow. Both countries have taken a number of initiatives to improve bilateral relations across a range of areas, without allowing existing differences to affect the overall development of their ties. China is set to emerge as India's leading trading partner in future and both countries, which face many common challenges, are exploring cooperative approaches to a range of issues including terrorism and protection of the environment.

India attaches great importance to close, cooperative and friendly relations with Japan, the second largest economy in Asia, and the other major pillar in Asia of our foreign policy. India's 'global partnership' with Japan reflects our common search for geopolitical, strategic and economic options in a rapidly changing world. In the next decade this relationship is set to become one of the most important factors in India's foreign policy matrix.

A Challenge and Opportunity

In the coming decade, India's foreign policy would have to contend with intensified engagement with not only the major powers but also emerging power centers as well as our immediate and extended neighbourhood. Demographic trends, policy choices and India's inherent societal strengths have come together to put India among the key players of this century. The world's perception of India, its capacities and its strengths has changed irreversibly. This is both a challenge and an opportunity for our foreign policy. India has to act, and more quickly than before, from a platform of increased self-assurance and responsibility to ensure that the country continues to enjoy a peaceful and supportive environment for pursuing her development goals and able to contribute, to the fashioning of a better world based on universal human values".

Independent Foreign Policy

In the first diplomatic visit in July 2008, after winning the trust vote in Parliament, External Affairs Minister Pranab Mukherjee left for Iran on a two-day visit. While the official context of the visit was to attend the Non-Aligned Movement's (NAM) ministerial conference, Mukherjee also had the objective to re-emphasise the country's independent foreign policy.

Mukherjee, during his visit between 29 and 30 July 2008, pushed for the $ 7.4 billion Iran-Pakistan-India gas pipeline, his presence also indicated India's commitment to NAM and its strong and vocal opposition to any military action against Iran.

All these put together sent out a signal to the international as well as the domestic audience that India's foreign policy remains independent, even it pursues the all-important Indo-US nuclear deal.

Mukherjee also used this opportunity to present India's case for global nuclear cooperation with some NAM countries that are also members of the International Atomic Energy Agency (IAEA) and Nuclear Suppliers Group (NSG) countries. Mukherjee met Iranian President Mahmoud Ahmadinejad, Foreign Minister Manouchehr Mottaki and

Petroleum Minister Gholamhossein Nozari to discuss a range of bilateral, regional and global issues. He met Saeed Jalili, Iran's chief nuclear negotiator and chief secretary of the Supreme National Security Council.

This was Mukherjee's first visit after the government decided to fast-track the nuclear-deal that could bring the two countries in closer economic and strategic embrace. The visit was closely watched in Washington, which wants to isolate Tehran over its suspected atomic weapon programme, and resents India's attempts to forge ties with Iran.

The pipeline that aspires to bring Iranian gas to India via Pakistan, figured high in the talks with Iran keen on resolving gas pricing and security issues with New Delhi. During his visit to India on 29 April, 2008, Ahmedinejad had set a 45-day deadline to sort out issues over the proposed pipeline, but there had been little progress since.

His visit also reaffirmed India's commitment to the ideals of non-alignment, which Washington views with reservation. "As one of the founders of NAM, India remains committed to its purposes and principles, and will continue its active and constructive engagement within it. India will work to further strengthen solidarity and cooperation among the member states of NAM which continues to play a crucial role in international affairs".

Indo-US Civil Nuclear Pact

Pranab Mukherjee as Foreign Minister dismissed the Opposition's demand to "mend or end" the Indo-US civil nuclear agreement and advised the Left to appreciate the changes in geopolitics post-Cold War.

Responding to leader of Opposition Jaswant Singh's stand that the government should take a call either way on the deal, Pranab said, "We are in a stage where neither we can mend it nor end it. We are in the dialogue stage," the remark illustrating the dilemma that the government found itself in, over the deal.

Mukherjee said that while talks with IAEA for India-specific safeguards have progressed, but no agreement had been inked. He promised to come to Parliament after the negotiations were over, while rejecting BJP's demand for a parliamentary scrutiny of the deal.

Left Parties Threat

The politbureau member of CPM Sitaram Yechury said that the joint military exercises with the US were a sign that India was now part of US's strategic designs for Asia. "If it falters on foreign policy, we will pull down the government. We cannot afford to be drawn into strategic tie-ups. We will not permit the government to succumb to US pressure," the CPM MP said.

He said if the CPM was still supporting the government it was only because of its belief that the foreign policy under BJP would be completely subservient to that of the US.

In a long reply, he also took on the Left for its criticism of the government for joint military exercises with the US. Seizing upon the Left's slanted approach towards military exercises, Mukherjee called strange, the logic that while military exercises with China and Russia were welcome, having similar partnership with the US would result in loss of sovereignty. Mukherjee said that India had conducted exercises with a whole host of countries – from Japan and Sri Lanka to Oman, Laos and Vietnam.

Mukherjee stressed that nothing had changed in the principles of India's foreign policy, but the world had moved on from the past and new formations emerged all the time, rendering old policies redundant.

"The type of foreign policy in the days of the Cold War has lost its relevance once the Cold War ended. There was a time when all our military equipment came from a particular country. New forces emerged, new realities emerged even during NAM heydays, and many other outfits like G-77 emerged, like the G-4 in United Nations Security Council now".

Pranab Meets George W Bush

At their meeting on 24th March, 2008 at the White House, President Bush and Minister Mukherjee discussed a wide range of bilateral and international issues, including the India-US civil nuclear initiative. National Security Advisor Stephen Hadley and Secretary of State Condoleezza Rice were also present at the meeting.

During their discussions, Mukherjee and Rice, agreed to "maintain the positive momentum" of the relationship generated particularly by the visits of Prime Minister Manmohan Singh to the US in July 2005, and that of President Bush to India in March 2006. "Several critical decisions were taken during those visits on a wide spectrum of issues important to both countries," Mukherjee noted.

"It will be our common endeavour to register progress on all of them," he said, addressing a joint press conference with Rice. "There is a broad overlap in our interests and objectives, and we intend to supplement our dialogue with a closer working-level interaction on a regular basis within the Ministry of External Affairs in India and the US State Department," he added.

The Minister said that he had discussed with the US leadership "the way forward on opening civil nuclear cooperation by India with the US and other partners as a critical element of our energy security".

The two leaders talked about what Rice described as "the deepening of our economic ties, of our defense cooperation, and the deepening of our dialogue about regional issues".

Mukherjee described his visit to the US as "very productive and fruitful" and expressed satisfaction with the progress in the relationship. "Two-way trade and investment between our two countries is growing along with our cooperation in agriculture, clean energy, environment, science and technology, health and education.

A similar momentum can also be seen in our defence ties, peaceful use of outer space, and other high-technology areas," he said.

"We believe that the India-US partnership is based on a bed rock of long-term commitments and a shared vision. My discussions with the US leaders, reinforced our view that the India-US relationship is robust and forward-leaning and answers to the interests of both countries. Based on a foundation of shared values and tangible mutual benefit, the India-US strategic partnership has grown from strength to strength. Our relations encompass a meaningful and regular political dialogue, vibrant economic and commercial interaction and collaboration over a wide spectrum of issues including energy, defense, space, science and technology, agriculture and education," Mukherjee said.

The two leaders also discussed climate change and the need for a successful conclusion of the Doha Development Round.

Eventful Tenure as an External Affairs Minister

Pranab Mukherjee's stint at the External Affairs Ministry in the UPA government was an eventful period, with major changes in the bilateral relations that India has had with the neighbouring and other foreign countries; as also global politico-economic and strategic alliances. A brief overview of the foreign policy initiatives during the period are discussed here.

India's foreign policy seeks to safeguard the country's enlightened self-interest. The primary objective of India's foreign policy is to promote and maintain a peaceful and stable external environment in which the domestic tasks of inclusive economic development and poverty alleviation can progress rapidly and without obstacles. Given the high priority attached by the Government of India to socio-economic development, India has a vital stake in a supportive external environment both in our region and globally. India, therefore, seeks a peaceful periphery and works for good neighbourly relations, in its extended neighbourhood. India's foreign policy also recognizes that the issues such as climate change and energy and food security that are crucial to India's transformation are global and require global cooperative solutions.

The past few years witnessed several positive developments, some significant successes, and a few major fresh threats to India's foreign policy.

Relations with Neighbours: India shares a common destiny with its neighbours. Relations with Bhutan developed further in the year of His Majesty's coronation and the introduction of democracy in Bhutan. India has strongly supported Nepal's transition to a democratic polity, and the restoration of democracy in Bangladesh. India has contributed to the reconstruction and development of Afghanistan. Apart from maintaining friendly and close bilateral relations with its neighbours, India has also worked for the evolution of SAARC into a result oriented organization that effectively promotes regional integration.

Sino-India Relations: Bilateral relations with China were further consolidated during 2008 with Manmohan Singh's official visit to China in January 2008 and External Affairs Minister Pranab Mukherjee's visit in June 2008. The situation along the India-China border remained peaceful while the boundary question continued to be addressed by the Special Representatives. Defence cooperation between the two countries has contributed to enhancement of mutual trust. China opened a new Consulate in Kolkata in September 2008 and earlier in June 2008 India had opened its Consulate in Guangzhou.

Indo-US Relations: A major development was the signing of the India-US Civil Nuclear Agreement in October 2008. The Agreement marked the end of three decades of technology denial in the nuclear field. Following the signing of this bilateral agreement, agreements for civil nuclear cooperation have been signed with France, Russia and Kazakhstan. The India-US strategic partnership was further consolidated by Manmohan Singh's visits to the US in September 2008, when he had a bilateral meeting with the US President George W Bush in Washington, and in November for the G-20 Summit. The US remained India's largest trading partner and source of technology and relations expanded in every field.

Relations with Russia: India's traditional friendship and strategic links with Russia were consolidated during the period. The President of the Russian Federation Dmitry Medvedev paid a state visit to India in December 2008 for the annual bilateral Summit. The year 2008 was observed in India as the 'Year of Russia'. The year 2009 was observed in Russia as the 'Year of India'. India is committed to further carry forward its strategic relations with Russia. India intends to build on its strong historical and cultural links with the Central Asian countries, and to engage more closely with this region by ensuring that cooperation with Central Asia receives greater substance and diversification.

India and European Union (EU): India has maintained and intensified its engagement with the EU, a strategic partner, as well as individual countries in Europe in diverse fields such as defence and security, nuclear and space, trade and investment, energy, climate change, science and technology, culture and education. The EU is today India's largest trading partner and one of our major sources of investment.

Other Countries and Multi-lateral Groupings

India continued to attach importance to its traditionally friendly and cooperative relations with African countries. A landmark event was the first ever India-Africa Forum Summit in April 2008 which adopted the Delhi Declaration and India-Africa Framework for Cooperation. Both documents together defined the future roadmap for cooperation between India and African countries. The Government of India's prestigious pan-African e-Network Project was inaugurated in New Delhi on 26th February, 2009 by External Affairs Minister Pranab Mukherjee.

India's efforts to cultivate stronger bonds with countries of the Latin American and Caribbean region have borne impressive results in recent years, with cross-sectoral dialogue at various levels and a framework of institutionalised mechanisms for mutually beneficial cooperation.

India's cooperation with the countries in West Asia and the Gulf region today reveal a contemporary nature and include the peaceful uses of outer space including the use of Indian launch vehicles. This region is also home to nearly five million Indian expatriates who have contributed significantly to the economic development of both India and the Gulf region.

India views cooperation with ASEAN, and the countries in the Asia-Pacific, as an important dimension of its diplomacy in the 21st century as reflected in India's "Look East Policy".

In 2009, India significantly expanded its network of economic and technical cooperation. India is ready to play a significant role in recently established forums such as IRC (India-Russia-China), BRIC (Brazil-Russia-India-China) and IBSA (India-Brazil-South Africa). India continues to engage in Mekong-Ganga Cooperation, G-15, and the G-8.

With its strong commitment to multilateralism, India has worked to strengthen the United Nations. India has supported proposals for the reform of the United Nations Security Council and revitalisation of the United Nations General Assembly. India would like to see the global institutions reflecting the new realities of the world order, taking into account the legitimate aspirations of developing countries and emerging powers.

Foreign Policy Challenges

Concurrent to these positive developments, India's foreign policy in 2008-09 faced new threats to India's security including the unsettled security situation in India's terror infested periphery and cross-border terrorism.

Pakistan

The composite dialogue process with Pakistan entered its fifth round in 2008-09. The dialogue was premised on Pakistan's stated commitment that it would not permit territory under its control to be used to support terrorism against India in any manner. However, Pakistan's inability to implement her commitments as evidenced by the terrorist attacks from Pakistan on the Indian Embassy in Kabul in July 2008 and on Mumbai in November 2008 effectively suspended the dialogue process.

The Mumbai attacks were universally condemned by the International community. Overwhelming evidence was presented to Pakistan and the world about the involvement of Pakistan-based terrorists in these attacks. Pakistan subsequently admitted for the first time that Pakistani nationals had hatched the conspiracy behind the attacks and carried them out. However, subsequent actions by Pakistan were dilatory and to obfuscate the issue, and are yet to bring the perpetrators to justice or to dismantle the infrastructure in Pakistan for terrorism against India.

Sri Lanka

In 2008, there were large scale military operations in Sri Lanka eliminating the LTTE's conventional military capability resulting in a major humanitarian crisis. India responded to the immediate humanitarian crisis by sending relief supplies and medical assistance to civilians and Internally Displaced Persons (IDPs). India also continued to stay engaged with Sri Lanka in support of a negotiated political settlement to the ethnic problem. As the situation in Sri Lanka enters a new phase, India will work for a peaceful settlement of the issues, within the framework of a united Sri Lanka, acceptable to all communities particularly the Tamils.

Global Economic Meltdown

The other major challenge during the year was the deteriorating international economic situation. As the international financial crisis became an economic crisis with recession in major Western economies and markets, the supportive international environment for India's growth changed rapidly. Despite this, the Indian economy grew by 6.7 per cent in 2008-09, and continues to be a factor of growth and stability in the world economy. India participated actively in international efforts to address the crisis, such as the G-20, to see that the concerns of developing countries were addressed. India also sought to ensure that international decision-making on global economic issues is democratised, to reflect present realities.

As the year 2008 ended, it was evident that cooperative global solutions are required to the major international issues which will affect India's future, such as the world economic crisis, international terrorism, general and nuclear disarmament, energy security, food security and sustainable development. As a responsible power, India remains an active and involved participant in the international effort to work out these solutions and will contribute to their success.

India Embraces Israel

The two countries are building a strong economic and defense relationship. Facing concerns over growing military capabilities in China and Pakistan, India is strengthening its relationships with other nations to build its own arsenal, to protect itself and its allies.

India maintains a strong partnership with the United States in developing its military capabilities and is working with Israel to improve relationships, particularly on the defense and strategic fronts.

India and Israel estimated bilateral trade between the two countries stands at $9 billion. The growing relationship between the two countries was highlighted by a recent visit to Israel by External Affairs Minister SM Krishna in 2012. Both the nations have to work out a strategy as to how we address ourselves to the scourge of international terrorism which has become the curse for the entire humanity.

Statement in Parliament on 26/11 Mumbai attack

The 2008 Mumbai attacks were eleven coordinated shooting and bombing attacks across Mumbai, India's largest city, by Islamist terrorists, who came from Pakistan. The attackers, allegedly received reconnaissance assistance before the attacks. Ajmal Kasab, the only attacker who was captured alive, later confessed during interrogation that the attacks were conducted with the support of Pakistan's ISI. The attacks, which drew widespread global condemnation, began on 26th November, and lasted until 29th November 2008, killing 164 people and wounding at least 308.

The External Affairs Minister Pranab Mukherjee condemned the dastardly terrorist attack on Mumbai and made a statement on the floor of the House.

On December 12, 2008 this House resolved, in a solemn Resolution that: "India shall not cease in her efforts until the terrorists and those who have trained, funded and abetted them are exposed and brought to justice".

Through the months of December, January and February, we have continued to use all means available and heightened our diplomatic activity to achieve the goals set for us, namely, to bring the perpetrators of the terrorist attacks on Mumbai to book, and to seek credible steps by Pakistan to ensure that there would no recurrence of such attacks.

The Mumbai attacks were a crime committed on India, the conspiracy for which was hatched, planned and organized in Pakistan. In our diplomatic effort, we made it clear to Pakistan and the international community:

Firstly, that the terrorist attack on Mumbai again underlines the grave threat that terrorism poses to peace and stability and therefore has to be seen in the context of the global challenge of terrorism. Terrorism emanating from

Pakistan is of course a direct threat to India, but it is equally a regional and a global threat.

Secondly, from our investigations the evidence was conclusive that the attack was planned, executed and launched from Pakistan territory, by Pakistanis and by elements based in Pakistan. The primary onus of responsibility lies on Pakistan to fully unveil the conspiracy, identify those guilty and act in a transparent and verifiable manner.

Thirdly, Mumbai was by no means the first or only terrorist attack on India linked to the infrastructure of terrorism in Pakistan. Nonetheless, with Mumbai a threshold was crossed and it was imperative that Pakistan act credibly against that infrastructure to prevent further attacks.

By early January 2009 our investigations had progressed to the point where the details could be shared with the international community and specific information, material and leads could be provided to the Government of Pakistan. On the 5th of January 2009 we conveyed to the Government of Pakistan material linking the Mumbai attack of 26-29 November, 2008 to elements in Pakistan. This included:

Materials from the interrogation of Mohammed Ajmal Kasab, the Pakistani national who is in police custody. Details of the terrorists' communication links with elements in Pakistan during the Mumbai attack. Detail of recovered weapons, equipment and other articles. Data retrieved from recovered GPS and satellite phones used by the terrorists.

A full dossier of the Mumbai attack was also prepared and forwarded to my counterpart Foreign Ministers. At the same time detailed briefings for all resident Heads of Missions in New Delhi were organised in the Ministry of External Affairs.

In our diplomatic exchanges, we conveyed our expectation that the Government of Pakistan promptly undertake further investigations in Pakistan and share the results with us so as to bring the perpetrators to justice, and that Pakistan would implement her bilateral, multilateral and international obligations to prevent terrorism in any manner from territory under her control.

It may be useful to recapitulate that this was the fourth formal and official communication that we had addressed to the Government of Pakistan on this issue. I had spoken on the telephone to the Foreign Minister of Pakistan on 28 November, 2008, when he was still in India. That conversation was followed up and formalised in writing on 29th (the next day) morning in the form of a speaking note. Secondly, on 1st December 2008 a formal demarche was made to the Government of Pakistan. Thirdly, on the 22nd December 2008, a letter from the Pakistani terrorist in our custody was officially forwarded to the Pakistan Government. And fourthly, on 5th January 2009 the dossier, with details I mentioned earlier, was given to the Government of Pakistan.

Pak Response

The Members are aware of the prevarication, denial, diversionary tactics and misplaced sense of victimhood which characterised Pakistan's reaction from early days after the Mumbai attack. Pakistan's political leadership did condemn the terrorist attack and promised us full cooperation in investigating the conspiracy in Pakistan. I do not discount in any way either their intent or their sincerity, but the fact remains that the overwhelming response of official Pakistan to the Mumbai attack was not appropriate to a terrorist attack where innocents were massacred in cold blood. Throughout the attempt was to divert attention from the terrorist attack and Pakistan's responsibilities to other issues.

On 16th January, 2009 the Government of Pakistan informed us that some action had been taken against the Jamat-ud-Dawa (JuD) in pursuance to its being listed by the UN as a terrorist organisation. Some of its members were placed on the Exit Control List, some arms licenses were cancelled, instructions issued to freeze the accounts of JuD, some activists of JuD were arrested and certain JuD publications were banned. We were also informed that with effect from 15th January, 2009, the Government of Pakistan had launched a formal inquiry into the Mumbai terrorist attack and that the Federal Investigation Agency had been given the responsibility of conducting the inquiry in accordance with the laws of Pakistan. Some details of the inquiry team were intimated to us.

In the afternoon of February 12, our High Commissioner in Pakistan was informed by the Pakistan Foreign Secretary of Pakistan's response to the dossier of material that we had made available to Pakistan on January 5 linking the terrorist attacks on Mumbai to perpetrators in Pakistan. This is a positive development. In their official response, the Pakistan authorities have admitted that elements in Pakistan were involved in the terrorist attacks on Mumbai. They are still in the process of investigating the attacks, and have taken certain actions including the arrest of some of those who were involved, and have filed a first information report in Pakistan.

Pakistan has also sought further information and material relating to the investigation. The Government of India will now examine the issues raised in Pakistan's response. After our examination, we will share whatever we can with Pakistan.

Members will appreciate that Government has constantly been guided by the two objective of ensuring that the perpetrators who planned, organised and trained the terrorists in Pakistan are brought to justice, and that the infrastructure of terrorism which exists in Pakistan is dismantled so that we prevent a recurrence of such attacks. The international community has also worked with us, using its influence on Pakistan to ensure that the terrorist infrastructure and the support provided to such elements is put to an end, since terrorism emanating out of Pakistan is a threat not only to us, but to the world. We will continue to review the situation including Pakistan's responses and will take further steps that we deem necessary in order to protect our people.

The threat of terrorism from Pakistan has emerged as a global menace and cancer. The major onus of responsibility to eliminate this threat rests on the Government of Pakistan. It is imperative that it act with sincerity and act effectively against the licence that terrorist groups enjoy in its territory. It is essential that the assurances given to us repeatedly at the highest level by Pakistan leaders are implemented as solemn commitments.

Since the 1st of December, 2008, the Composite Dialogue process with Pakistan has been at a pause. No meeting has taken place and neither are any scheduled. It is also the case that the substantial gains in the process of normalisation, which were achieved in the last four or five years are at grave risk. As Members are aware, the dialogue and normalisation process was premised on commitments given by Pakistan that territory under its control would not be used for terrorism in any manner.

We are at a point in our relationship where the authorities in Pakistan itself have to choose the kind of relationship that they want with India in the future. Much depends on actions in the Mumbai case reaching their logical conclusion. I must underline that we have no quarrel with the people of Pakistan. We wish them well and we do not think that they should be held responsible or face the consequences of this situation. We have, therefore, consciously, and after due deliberation, not thought it necessary or fit to curtail people to people contacts, trains and road links.

Chapter - VI

Role in Civil Nuclear Energy Initiative

A Landmark Achievement

Pranab Mukherjee did a brilliant job to formulate the India's civil nuclear energy initiative when he was the External Affairs Minister in 2008. He said that India's civil nuclear initiative that has seen the lifting of three decades of sanctions is "a landmark achievement" that would help the country "occupy its well-deserved position in the comity of nations".

The initiative has seen the Nuclear Suppliers Group (NSG) granting an India-specific waiver to enable the resumption of nuclear commerce after a three-decade hiatus and the signing of cooperation agreements with the US and France. India will "have the right to reprocess the spent nuclear material that we obtain from our international partners. He added that "We will also be setting up a new national reprocessing facility, and taking other steps necessary to operationalise these agreements, and realise the full potential of the civil nuclear initiative".

Pranab also announced that India would sign a nuclear cooperation agreement with Russia when President Dmitry

Medvedev visits New Delhi in December, 2008. India and Russia signed a landmark agreement on civil nuclear cooperation on December 5 in the same year to give it a further boost. After the historical pact duly signed between two countries, the Prime Minister of India addressed a joint press conference with Russian President Dmitry Medvedev in New Delhi. He said that Moscow would build four additional atomic reactors in the Koodankulam nuclear plant in Tamil Nadu.

"The civil nuclear initiative not only allows us to meet out future energy requirements in a sustainable manner but is also one which acknowledges India's growing role in global affairs".

Mukherjee's this statement was seen as an attempt on the part of the government to blunt the Left parties' move to corner the government on the India-US nuclear deal in parliament.

Referring to the India specific safeguards agreement with the International Atomic Energy Association (IAEA), he said: "We will bring the agreement into force and offer facilities for safeguards in a phased manner in accordance with the provisions of the Safeguards Agreement and in keeping with our Separation Plan. "We are now in the process of getting visas by engaging with our international partners, to negotiate and finalise bilateral co-operation agreements".

Indo-US Civil Nuclear Agreement

The 123 Agreement signed between the United States of America and the Republic of India is known as the Indo-US Civil Nuclear Agreement or Indo-US nuclear deal. The framework for this agreement was a July 18, 2005, joint statement by Indian Prime Minister Manmohan Singh and the then US President George W Bush, under which India agreed to separate its civil and military nuclear facilities and to place all its civil nuclear facilities under International Atomic Energy Agency (IAEA) safeguards and, in exchange, the United States agreed to work toward full civil nuclear cooperation with India. This US-India deal took more than three years to come to fruition, as it had to go through several complex stages, including amendment of US domestic law, specially the Atomic Energy Act of 1954, a civil-military nuclear Separation Plan in India, an India-IAEA safeguards (inspections) agreement and the grant of an exemption for India by the Nuclear Suppliers Group, an export-control cartel that had been formed mainly in response to India's first nuclear test in 1974. In its final shape, the deal places under permanent safeguards those nuclear facilities that India has identified as "civil" and permits broad civil nuclear cooperation, while excluding the transfer of "sensitive" equipment and technologies, including civil enrichment and reprocessing items even under IAEA safeguards. On August 18, 2008 the IAEA Board of Governors approved, and on February 2, 2009, India signed an India-specific safeguards agreement with the IAEA. Once India brings this agreement into force, inspections will begin in a phased manner on the 35 civilian nuclear installations India has identified in its Separation Plan. The deal is seen as a watershed in US-India relations and introduces a new aspect to international non-proliferation efforts. On August 1, 2008, the IAEA approved the safeguards agreement with India, after which the United States approached the Nuclear Suppliers Group (NSG) to grant a waiver to India to commence civilian nuclear trade. The 45-nation NSG granted the waiver to India on September 6, 2008 allowing it to access civilian nuclear technology and fuel from other countries. The implementation of this waiver made India the only known country with nuclear weapons which is not a party to the Non Proliferation Treaty (NPT) but is still allowed to carry out nuclear commerce with the rest of the world.

The US House of Representatives passed the bill on September 28, 2008. Two days later, India and France inked a similar nuclear pact making France the first country to have such an agreement with India. On October 1, 2008 the US Senate also approved the civilian nuclear agreement allowing India to purchase nuclear fuel and technology from the United States. US President, George W Bush, signed the legislation on the Indo-US nuclear deal, approved by the US Congress, into law, now called the United States-India Nuclear Cooperation Approval and Non-proliferation Enhancement Act, on October 8, 2008. The agreement was signed by the then Indian External Affairs Minister Pranab Mukherjee and his counterpart, the then Secretary of State Condoleezza Rice, on October 10.

The Hyde Act

The Henry J Hyde United States-India Peaceful Atomic Energy Cooperation Act of 2006, also known as the Hyde Act, is the US domestic law that modifies the requirements of Section 123 of the US Atomic Energy Act, to permit nuclear cooperation with India, and in particular to negotiate a 123 Agreement to operationalise the 2005 Joint Statement. As a domestic US law, the Hyde Act is binding on the United States. The Hyde Act cannot be binding on India's sovereign decisions, although it can be construed as prescriptive for future US reactions. As per the Vienna convention, an international treaty such as the 123 agreement cannot be superseded by an internal law such as the Hyde Act.

The 123 agreement defines the terms and conditions for bilateral civilian nuclear cooperation, and requires separate approvals by the US Congress and by Indian cabinet ministers. According to the Nuclear Power Corporation of India, the agreement will help India meet its goal of adding 25,000 MW of nuclear power capacity through imports of nuclear reactors and fuel by 2020.

After the terms of the 123 agreement were concluded on July 27, 2007, it ran into trouble because of stiff opposition in India from the Communist allies of the ruling United Progressive Alliance. The government survived a confidence vote in the parliament on July 22, 2008 by 275–256 votes in the backdrop of defections by some parties. The deal also had faced opposition from non-proliferation activists, anti-nuclear organizations, and some states within the Nuclear Suppliers Group. In February 2008 then US Secretary of State Condoleezza Rice said that any agreement would be "consistent with the obligations of the Hyde Act". The bill was signed on October 8, 2008.

Rationale behind the Agreement

The proposed civil nuclear agreement implicitly recognises India's "de facto" status even without signing the NPT. The Bush administration justifies a nuclear pact with India because it is important in helping to advance the non-proliferation framework by formally recognising India's strong non-proliferation record even though it has not signed the NPT. The former Under Secretary of State of Political Affairs, Nicholas Burns, one of the architects of the Indo-US nuclear deal, when asked, whether the US would offer a similar nuclear deal to Pakistan on the lines of the Indo-US deal. said "India's trust, its credibility, the fact that it has promised to create a state-of-the-art facility, monitored by the IAEA, to begin a new export control regime in place, (as also) because it has not proliferated the nuclear technology, we can't say that about Pakistan,"

Mohammed El Baradei, former head of the International Atomic Energy Agency, which would be in charge of inspecting India's civilian reactors, has praised the deal as "it would also bring India closer as an important partner in the non-proliferation regime".

Economic Considerations

Financially, the US also expects that such a deal could spur India's economic growth and bring in $150 billion in the next decade for nuclear power plants, of which the US wants a share. It is India's stated objective, to increase the production of nuclear power generation from its present capacity of 4,000 MWe to 20,000 MWe in the next decade. However, the developmental economic advising firm Dalberg, which advises the IMF and the World Bank, has done its own analysis of the economic value of investing in nuclear power development in India. Their conclusion, however, is that for the next 20 years such investments are likely to be far less valuable economically or environmentally than a variety of other measures to increase electricity production in India. They have noted that US nuclear vendors cannot sell any reactors to India unless and until India caps third party liabilities or establishes a credible liability pool to protect US firms from being sued in the case of an accident or a terrorist act of sabotage against nuclear plants. Although India's parliament passed The Civil Liability for Nuclear Damages bill on August 25, 2010, the legislation does not meet international standards for nuclear liability as set forth in the Convention on Supplementary Compensation for Nuclear Damage, because it allows the operator to sue the supplier in case of an accident due to technical defects in the plant. After the Fukushima Daiichi Nuclear Power Plant in Japan, issues relating to the safety of operating nuclear power plants, compensation in the event of a radiation-leak accident, disaster clean-up costs, operator responsibility and supplier liability have once again come into the spot-light.

Strategic

Since the end of the Cold War, the Pentagon, along with certain US ambassadors such as Robert Blackwill, has requested increased strategic ties with India and a de-hyphenization of Pakistan with India, i.e., having separate policies toward India and Pakistan rather than just an "India-Pakistan" policy. The United States also sees India as a viable counter-weight to the growing influence of China and a potential client and job creator.

While India is self-sufficient in thorium, possessing 25 per cent of the world's known and economically viable thorium, it possesses a meager 1 per cent of the similarly calculated global uranium reserves.

Indian support for cooperation with the US centers on the issue of obtaining a steady supply of sufficient energy for the economy to grow. Indian opposition to the pact centers on the concessions that would need to be made, as well as the likely de-prioritisation of research into a thorium fuel cycle if uranium becomes readily available, given the well-understood utilisation of uranium in a nuclear fuel cycle.

Opposition to the Indo-US Civil Agreement in India

The Indo-US civil nuclear agreement was met with stiff opposition by some political parties and activists in India. Although many mainstream political parties including the Congress supported the deal along with regional parties like Dravida Munnetra Kazhagam, Rashtriya Janata Dal, its realisation ran into difficulties in the face of stiff political opposition in India. In November 2007, former Indian Military chiefs, bureaucrats and scientists drafted a letter to Members of Parliament expressing their support for the deal. However, opposition and criticism continued at political levels. The Samajwadi Party (SP) which was with the Left Front in opposing the deal changed its stand after discussing with ex-president of India and scientist Dr APJ Abdul Kalam. The SP then supported the government and the deal.

Prime Minister Manmohan Singh's statement in Parliament was totally at variance with the Bush Administration's communication to the House Foreign Affairs Committee, which says India will not be allowed to stockpile such nuclear fuel stocks as to undercut American leverage to re-impose sanctions. To drive home this point, it says the 123 Agreement is not inconsistent with the Hyde Act's stipulation—the little-known 'Barack Obama Amendment' - that the supply of nuclear fuel should be "commensurate with reasonable operating requirements". The 'strategic reserve' that is crucial to India's nuclear program is, therefore, a non-starter. Furthermore, the agreement, as a result of its compliance with the Hyde Act, contained a direct linkage between shutting down US nuclear trade with India and any potential future Indian nuclear weapons test, a point that was factually inconsistent with explicit reassurances made on this subject by Prime

Minister Manmohan Singh, during final parliamentary debate on the nuclear deal. As professor Brahma Chellaney, an expert in strategic affairs and one of the authors of the Indian Nuclear Doctrine, explained:

"While the Hyde Act's bar on Indian testing is explicit, the one in the NSG waiver is implicit, yet unmistakable. The NSG waiver is overtly anchored in NSG Guidelines Paragraph 16, which deals with the consequence of "an explosion of a nuclear device". The waiver's Section 3(e) refers to this key paragraph, which allows a supplier to call for a special NSG meeting, and seek termination of cooperation, in the event of a test or any other "violation of a supplier-recipient understanding". The recently leaked Bush administration letter to Congress has cited how this Paragraph 16 rule will effectively bind India to the Hyde Act's conditions on the pain of a US-sponsored cut-off of all multilateral cooperation. India will not be able to escape from the US-set conditions by turning to other suppliers".

Indian Parliament vote

On July 9, 2008, India formally submitted the safeguards agreement to the IAEA. This development came after the Prime Minister Manmohan Singh returned from the 34th G8 summit meeting in Hokkaido, Japan, where he met with US President George W Bush. On June 19, 2008, News media reported that Prime Minister Manmohan Singh threatened to resign his position, if the Left Front, whose support was crucial for the ruling United Progressive Alliance to prove its majority in the Parliament, continued to oppose the nuclear deal and he described their stance as irrational and reactionary. External Affairs Minister Pranab Mukherjee's earlier statement said "I cannot bind the government if we lose our majority," implying that United Progressive Alliance government would not put its signature on any deal with IAEA if it lost the majority in either a 'opposition-initiated no-confidence motion' or if failing to muster a vote of confidence in Indian Parliament after being told to prove its majority by the president. On July 8, 2008, Prakash Karat announced that the Left Front is withdrawing its support to the government over the decision by the government to go ahead on the United States-India Peaceful Atomic Energy Cooperation Act. The Left Front had been a staunch advocate of not proceeding with this deal citing national interests.

On July 22, 2008 the UPA faced its first confidence vote in the Lok Sabha after the Communist Party of India (Marxist) led Left Front withdrew support over India approaching the IAEA for Indo-US nuclear deal. The UPA won the confidence vote with 275 votes to the opposition's 256, (10 members abstained from the vote) to record a 19-vote victory.

IAEA approval

The IAEA Board of Governors approved the safeguards agreement on August 1, 2008, and the 45-state Nuclear Suppliers Group next had to approve a policy allowing nuclear cooperation with India. US President Bush can then make the necessary certifications and seek final approval by the US Congress. There were objections from Pakistan, Iran, Ireland, Norway, Switzerland and Austria at the IAEA meeting.

NSG waiver

On September 6, 2008 India was granted the waiver at the NSG meeting held in Vienna, Austria. The consensus was arrived at after overcoming misgivings expressed by Austria, Ireland and New Zealand and is an unprecedented step in giving exemption to a country which has not signed the NPT and the Comprehensive Test Ban Treaty (CTBT). The Indian team, which worked on the deal, included Manmohan Singh, Pranab Mukherjee, Shivshankar Menon, Shyam Saran, MK Narayanan, Anil Kakodkar, Ravi Grover, and DB Venkatesh Varma.

World Support and Opposition

The deal had initial support from the United States, the United Kingdom, France, Japan, Russia, and Germany. After some initial opposition, there were reports of Australia, Switzerland, and Canada expressing their support for the deal. Selig S Harrison, a former South Asia bureau chief of *The Washington Post*, has said the deal may represent a tacit recognition of India as a nuclear weapon state, while former US Undersecretary of State for Arms Control and International Security Robert Joseph said "US State Department made it very clear that we will not recognise India as a nuclear-weapon state".

Norway, Austria, Brazil, and Japan all warned that their support for India at the IAEA did not mean that they would not express reservations at the NSG. New Zealand, which is a member of the NSG but not of the IAEA Board of Governors, cautioned that its support should not be taken for granted. Ireland, which launched the non-proliferation treaty process in 1958 and signed it first in 1968, doubted India's nuclear trade agreement with the US-Russia, a potentially large nuclear supplier to India, expressed reservations about transferring enrichment and reprocessing technology to India. China argued the agreement constituted "a major blow to the international non-proliferation regime". New Zealand said it would like to see a few conditions written in to the waiver: the exemption ceasing if India conducts nuclear tests, India signing the International Atomic Energy Agency's (IAEA) additional protocol, and placing limits on the scope of the technology that can be given to India and which could relate to nuclear weapons. Austria, Ireland, the Netherlands, Switzerland and Scandinavian countries proposed similar amendments. The nuclear deal was opposed by former US president Jimmy Carter, who opined that the US would be making "a dangerous deal with India".

After the first NSG meeting in August 2008, diplomats noted that up to 20 of the 45 NSG states tabled conditions similar to the Hyde Act for India's waiver to do business with the NSG. "There were proposals on practically every paragraph," a European diplomat said. A group of seven NSG members suggested including some of the provisions of the US Hyde Act in the final waiver. Daryll Kimball, executive director of the Washington-based Arms Control Association, said the NSG should at a minimum "make clear that nuclear trade with India shall be terminated if it resumes testing for any reason. If India cannot agree to such terms, it suggests that India is not serious about its nuclear test moratorium pledge".

Reactions Following the Waiver

After India was granted the waiver on September 6, the United Kingdom said that the NSG's decision would make a "significant contribution" to global energy and climate security. The US National Security Council spokesman Gordon Johndroe said, "This is a historic achievement that strengthens global non-proliferation principles while assisting India to meet its energy requirements in an environmentally friendly manner. The United States thanks the participating governments in the NSG for their outstanding efforts and cooperation to welcome India into the global non-proliferation community. We especially appreciate the role Germany played as chair to move this process forward". New Zealand praised the NSG consensus and said that it got the best possible deal with India. One of India's strongest allies Russia said in a statement, "We are convinced that the exemption made for India reflects Delhi's impeccable record in the non-proliferation sphere and will guarantee the peaceful uses of nuclear exports to India". Australian Foreign Minister Stephen Smith said that the NSG granted waiver because of "India's rise as a global power" and added, "If such a request was made for another country, I don't think it would have been cleared by the NSG members". During his visit to India in September 2008, Smith said that Australia "understood and respected India's decision not to join the Non-Proliferation Treaty". German

Foreign Ministry spokesman Jens Ploetner called India a "special case" and added, "Does this agreement send an approving message to Iran? No, it absolutely does not".

Indian Reactions

PM Manmohan Singh visited Washington DC on September 26, 2008 to celebrate the conclusion of the agreement with US President George W Bush. He also visited France to convey his appreciation for the country's stance. External Affairs Minister Pranab Mukherjee expressed his deep appreciation for India's allies in the NSG, especially the United States, United Kingdom, France, Russia, Germany, South Africa and Brazil for helping India achieve NSG's consensus on the nuclear deal.

Bharatiya Janata Party's Yashwant Sinha, who also formerly held the post of India's External Affairs Minister, criticised the Indian government's decision to seek NSG's consensus and remarked that "India has walked into the non-proliferation trap set by the US, we have given up our right to test nuclear weapons forever, it has been surrendered by the government". However, another prominent member of the same party and India's former National Security Advisor Brajesh Mishra supported the development at the NSG and said that the waiver granted made "no prohibition" on India to conduct nuclear tests in the future.

A leading advocate of the agreement was India's most eminent strategic affairs analyst K Subrahmanyam, also known for his long and controversial championing of an Indian nuclear deterrent. He argued that the convergence of strategic interests between the two nations forced such a remarkable gesture from the US, overturning its decades-long stand on non-proliferation, and that it would be unwise on India's part to spurn such an overture. He also argued that not recognising new geo-political realities would be even more foolhardy on the part of the Indian elite.

Former President of India and noted Indian scientist, APJ Abdul Kalam, also supported the agreement and remarked that New Delhi may break its "voluntary moratorium" on further nuclear tests in "supreme national interest". However, analyst MK Bhadrakumar demurred. He said that the consensus at NSG was achieved on the "basis" of Pranab Mukherjee's commitment to India's voluntary moratorium on nuclear testing and by doing so India has entered into a "multilateral commitment" bringing it within "the ambit of the CTBT and NPT".

Consideration by US Congress

The Bush Administration told Congress in January 2008 that the United States may cease all cooperation with India if India detonates a nuclear explosive device. The Administration further said it was not its intention to assist India in the design, construction or operation of sensitive nuclear technologies through the transfer of dual-use items. The statements were considered sensitive in India because debate over the agreement in India could have toppled the government of Prime Minister Manmohan Singh. The State Department had requested they remain secret even though they were not classified. Secretary of State Condoleezza Rice also previously told the House Foreign Affairs Panel in public testimony that any agreement would "have to be completely consistent with the obligations of the Hyde Act". Assistant Secretary of State for South and Central Asian Affairs Richard Boucher and the Former Assistant Secretary of State for Legislative Affairs Jeffrey Bergner also said the agreement would be in conformity with the Hyde Act.

On September 28, 2008 the US House of Representatives voted 298 to 117, to approve the Indo-US nuclear deal. On October 1, 2008 the US Senate voted 86 to 13 to approve the Indo-US nuclear deal. The Arms Control Association said the agreement fails to make clear that an Indian nuclear test would prompt the US to cease nuclear trade; however, Secretary of State Condoleezza Rice said that any nuclear test by India would result in the "most serious consequences," including automatic cut-off of US cooperation as well as a number of other sanctions.

After Senate approval, US President George W Bush said the deal would "strengthen our global nuclear non-proliferation efforts, protect the environment, create jobs, and assist India in meeting its growing energy needs in a responsible manner". Then-US presidential candidates Barack Obama and John McCain, as well as the then Vice Presidential candidate Joe Biden, voted in support of the bill.

Formal Signing of the Deal

There was speculation the Indo-US deal would be signed on October 4, 2008 when US Secretary of State Condoleezza Rice was in India. The deal was to be inked by Indian External Affairs Minister Pranab Mukherjee and US Secretary of State Condoleezza Rice. The two leaders were to sign the deal at 2 pm at the Hyderabad House in New Delhi. But Mukherjee announced that India would wait for the US President to sign the 123 agreement legislation first into law and address India's concerns on fuel supply guarantees and the legal standing of the 123 agreement in the accompanying signing statement.

Rice was aware of the Indian decision before she left Washington. But she was very hopeful, that the deal would be signed as the US state department had said that the President's signature was not prerequisite for Rice to ink the deal. Rice had earlier said that there were still a number of administrative details to be worked out, even as she insisted that the US would abide by the Hyde Act on the testing issue:

"There are a lot of administrative details that have to be worked out. This (the deal) was only passed in our Congress two days ago. The President is looking forward to signing the bill, sometime, I hope, very soon, because we'll want to use it as an opportunity to thank all of the people who have been involved in this," said Rice.

In Washington, a Senate Democratic aide said that such a delay was not that unusual because legislation needed to be carefully reviewed before being sent to the White House.

US President George W Bush signed the legislation on the Indo-US nuclear deal into law on 8th October, 2008. The new law, called the United States-India Nuclear Cooperation Approval and Non-proliferation Enhancement Act, was signed by President Bush at a brief White House function in the presence of the Secretary of State Condoleezza Rice, Energy Secretary Samuel Bodman, Vice-President Dick Cheney and the Indian Ambassador to the US Ronen Sen, besides a large gathering of other dignitaries. The final administrative aspect of the deal was completed, after Secretary of State Condoleezza Rice and External Affairs Minister Pranab Mukherjee, signed the bilateral instruments of the 123 Agreement in Washington on 10 October, 2008, paving the way for making the deal operational, between the two countries.

Chapter - VII

As Finance Minister

First Stint as FM

Pranab Mukherjee's first stint as the Finance Minister of India was during the Indira Gandhi government in 1982. He presented his first annual budget in 1982-83.

When Pranab Mukherjee took the charge as the Finance Minister of India, Indian economy was in complete mess. India's foreign exchange reserves were not sufficient to meet the requirement. Deficit financing was so high in terms of the percentage of the GDP that it could not be sustained. In any case, lenders were no longer willing to finance the deficit. And, there was real danger of the country defaulting on its foreign loan repayments.

Mukherjee sought a free hand from Prime Minister Indira Gandhi, and at that time Manmohan Singh was the Governor of the RBI, who became the Finance Minister in 1991 and emphasised the need for globalisation with new foreign direct investments.

Finance Minister's first mission was to address the fundamental problems of the Indian economy, so as to create an environment for businesses to grow and to let the inherent entrepreneurial skill of the countrymen to be leveraged. He was very forthright in saying, that he wanted the government off the back of the Indian people to leave them alone to work and provide strength to the economy. When he went ahead to release the Indian economy from the vice-like grip of a corruption and delay-generating bureaucracy, there were protests not only from those whose powers were being curbed but also Members of Parliament, even from his own party who did not see eye-to-eye with what he was doing.

Mixed Economy

Pranab Mukherjee has always been emphatic about needs of a strong public sector as also a strong and vibrant private sector. This idea of a mixed economy for India was held by India's first Prime Minister, Pandit Jawaharlal Nehru.

Pranab Da agreed that there must be some form of control and rationing when demand far exceeds supply. However, he was convinced that the 'license-quota-permit-raj' creates chances for corruption, leading to dampening effect on enterprise.

He acknowledged the progress made by certain economies of East and South East Asia in the seventies and the eighties, South Korea being a shining example of achieving the status of a developed economy in within one generation. In the same period, the Central Planning in India did not deliver similar economic growth rate achieved by these economies. It remained the sole objective of Mukherjee to make India a major global economic power.

His first term as Finance Minister was noteworthy for India not withdrawing the last one billion dollar installment of an International Monetary Fund (IMF) loan, as he managed to turn the Indian economy around and was adjudged as one of the best five finance ministers of the world, in 1984 by a New York Journal, '*Euromoney*'.

Second Stint as Finance Minister

In the second term government of Manmohan Singh, he again became the Finance Minister. The immediate aftermath of the traumatic 26/11 attack on Mumbai in 2008 left in its wake a brutalized collective psyche of Indians. Incumbent Home Minister Shivraj Patil was sacked and Finance Minister P Chidambaram was shifted to the ministry of home affairs. Chidambaram's move came at an extremely sensitive time, for the world economy was in the throes of a massive meltdown triggered by the demise of iconic investment banks in the US. One bank after another capitulated - Bear Sterns, Lehman Brothers - while Goldman Sachs was bailed out by Warren Buffet. There was tumult in global markets and India was no exception.

Once Chidambaram was saddled with his new responsibility, PM Manmohan Singh took additional charge of finance. On December 7, 2008, deputy chairman of Plan Panel - Montek Singh Ahluwalia unveiled a massive economic stimulus package to drive consumption and demand, so that the wheels keep moving. The building blocks of this package were put in place by Chidambaram in conjunction with department of economic affairs secretary Ashok Chawla, chief economic adviser Arvind Virmani, with inputs from Montek Singh. The first of these stimulus packages went a long way in alleviating the woes of a beleaguered nation. This catalyst, adrenalised the economy, and kept it going. By January 2009, Pranab Mukherjee had taken additional charge of finance ministry. In February with general elections looming large on the radar, Pranab Babu presented an interim budget. He supplemented it in July 2009 with the Union budget.

Affection for Sonia Gandhi

Mukherjee has tremendous admiration for Indira's daughter-in-law especially for keeping national interest above anything else and apt party management. It's now an oft-repeated story in the corridors of power that Mukherjee's return to the finance ministry in 2009 was primarily because Sonia Gandhi wanted him there, while Prime Minister Manmohan Singh was initially toying with the idea of having someone like Montek Singh Ahluwalia.

A budget was to be presented within a month of his taking over the finance portfolio and Mukherjee wasted no time in meeting the Congress President for guidance. When he asked what all she wants to see in the budget, Sonia Gandhi reportedly told Mukherjee, "More than economic jargon, I know one thing: I am for the poor people of our country. Do something for them". Consequently, Mukherjee's budget saw huge rise in expenses in the social sector schemes.

On July 6, 2009, he presented the government's annual budget. In it, he announced many tax reforms, such as the scrapping of the 'irritant' Fringe Benefits Tax and the Commodities Transaction Tax. He announced that the Finance Ministry was well on track to implement Goods and Services Tax, a proposal that has been praised by major corporate executives, and economists. He also expanded funding for social sector schemes, like the National Rural Employment Guarantee Act (NREGA), girl's literacy, and health care. Also, he expanded infrastructure programmes like the National Highway Development Programme, expansion of electricity coverage, and the Jawaharlal Nehru National Urban Renewal Mission (JNURM). However, many people expressed concern about the rising fiscal deficit, the highest since 1991. Mukherjee believed that the expansion in government spending was only temporary, and he said that the government was committed to the principle of fiscal prudence. He presented the 2009 Union budget as well as 2010 and 2011 Union budgets.

The 2010-11 budgets include the country's first explicit target to cut public debt as a proportion of GDP and he targeted a budget deficit reduction to 4.1 per cent of GDP in fiscal year 2012-13, from 6.5 per cent in 2008-09.

Global Recession

Finance Minister Pranab Mukherjee was rated as one of the best minds in the Manmohan Singh government and has succeeded in steering the Indian economy to one of the fastest growth rates in the world, at a time when the western economies had collapsed, and soaring international prices of crude and other essential imports fuelled domestic inflation.

He also placed more money in the hands of consumers by scaling down income tax rates, and cut excise duties on goods such as cars, refrigerators and TV sets, so that prices remained within the reach of buyers and factories could keep up production.

Various tax concessions, given to exporters helped them to keep afloat and earn precious foreign exchange, as they were able to diversify into markets outside Europe and the USA, where the demand for Indian goods had crashed, in the wake of the economic meltdown.

It goes to his credit that Foreign Direct Investment (FDI) has continued to flow into the country, despite the slowdown worldwide and the country had ample foreign exchange reserves to finance imports at a time when international oil prices are going through the roof.

The most complicated of policy decisions confronting the UPA government - whether it be related to land acquisition, telecom, mining, the oil sector or the need for sugar exports - are always passed on to a group of ministers, invariably headed by Mukherjee, to take the final call. His sagacity is much needed at this crucial juncture, when the Euro Zone jitters are impacting the Indian economy adversely.

Steps for Improving Economy

Finance Minister Pranab Mukherjee said that the government would announce certain measures in consultation with the Reserve Bank of India (RBI) to improve the country's economy that was showing signs of weakness.

Speaking of the economy on his last visit to Kolkata as the Union Finance Minister, Mukherjee said, "I would like to say GDP growth is at 6.5 per cent. There is inflationary pressure on the economy; there is depreciation of the rupee. These are no doubt signs of weakness in Indian economy," and added, "I am concerned but I am not depressed".

He thinks when the global economy is in turmoil, "then no country can expect that there will be pocket of development and particularly a large economy like India which is the third largest in terms of purchasing power parity cannot remain insulated from external factors".

The rupee has lost over 20 per cent against the US dollar in the last one year. It has weakened to over Rs 56 to a dollar, exerting inflationary pressure on the economy, particularly with regard to crude oil imports. The stock market has lost ground and industrial growth has slipped to 0.1 per cent in first quarter of the year. However, Mukherjee said the Indian economy is resilient and its fundamentals were strong.

He said the period from January to June 6, 2012 saw an inflow of FII money to the tune of $8 billion, as against negative flow in 2011. "FDI stood at $46-48 billion which is higher than last fiscal," Mukherjee said.

Steps to Improve India's Credit Rating

Pranab Mukherjee believes that the Government of India is all set to take a slew of measures to streamline and improve its growth rate figure consequent to Fitch and Standard and Poor's downgrading the country's credit rating.

In mid 2012 Fitch Ratings cut its credit outlook for India to negative from stable, nearly two months after rival Standard and Poor's made a similar call, citing risks that India's growth outlook could deteriorate, if policymaking and governance don't improve.

The agency estimated general government debt for India of 66 per cent of GDP at the end of the most recent fiscal year, compared with a median of 39 per cent for BBB-rated countries. India's economy grew just 5.3 per cent in the March quarter in 2012, the weakest in nine years.

Reserve Bank of India unexpectedly left interest rates on hold, sending bonds, stocks and the rupee lower. The rupee weakened further to Rs 56 per dollar from around 55.82 before the Fitch statement. Bond yields were range-bound, while stocks were already shut for the day.

Fitch maintained its BBB-rating, the lowest investment grade.

"I have taken note of the comments, observations and ratings of Fitch. In certain areas we are yet to take appropriate measures. But we have already started taking appropriate measures. There have been some improvement in the inflow of FII (foreign institutional investment), FDI (foreign direct investment) and certain steps have been taken in the areas of external commercial borrowing, providing long term finance for infrastructure by creating the infrastructure debt fund. These have started yielding results but it will take some time," said Pranab Mukherjee.

Earlier, Standards and Poor (S and P) had noted that India could become the first of the BRIC (Brazil, Russia, India, China) economies, to lose its investment-grade status, prompting an angry response from the government.

Basic Fundamentals are Strong

Pranab Mukherjee said the basic fundamentals of Indian economy are strong and there is resilience of the Indian economy. There has been a positive inflow not outflow. It is around eight billion US dollars. During the calendar year of 2011, there was outflow not inflow. The second point is gross FDI is also more compared to the year of 2010-11.

Pranab Promises Fast Policy Action

As Pranab gets ready to move to Raisina Hills, he had some encouraging words for India Inc, which has been critical over the policy paralysis at the capital.

Mukherjee said, "Even as the Centre was doing its bit to bring the economy back on growth path, the Reserve Bank of India could also lower interest rates".

He said the Centre had been taking various steps to address concerns expressed not only by Corporate India, but also international credit rating agencies to dispel the recurrent talk of policy inaction by the Centre and the North Block.

During a seminar organised by Assocham, the Finance Minister said he was aware of the challenges India was facing and expressed the optimism that measures taken by the government would yield results soon.

The Finance Minister also had a word of advice for India Inc. Admitting that there was a 'negative sentiment'' when it came to investment, he said the country had to find its own solution to the problem.

Mukherjee said "My only request to leaders and captains of industry is that we should take note of these areas of difficulty, but we will have to find our own solutions. I believe industry has the resilience, the economy has the resilience and we are competent to rise to the task of meeting grave challenges''.

He added that there was a need to encourage people to invest in market instruments. The Minister regretted that people were investing in gold with the expectation that the value of their investment would appreciate. "Quantum of import of gold ... is a clear indication (that) large section of community...want (to) investment in dead asset only with expectation that its value would appreciate," he said.

Financial Security and International Interdependence

While distinguishing between 'financial security' and the notion of 'financial stability', Pranab Mukherjee accepted the fact that growing interdependence among states has led to a fair amount of uncertainty in the international economy. Expansions in international trade have turned the problems of otherwise smaller countries into systemic risks, making the relevance of country size somewhat redundant. In view of the contemporary trends in global economy, Mukherjee revisited the merits of financial regulation to sustain growth within the scope of stability and financial security.

Steps to Improve FDI Inflow

According to Mukherjee "There is some improvement in FDI and FII inflows". The steps taken by the government to relax External Commercial Borrowings (ECB) norms and creation of Infrastructure Debt Fund (IDF) too were yielding results.

Mukherjee had said in a statement, "Fitch has primarily relied on older data, and has ignored the recent positive trends in the Indian economy".

According to the statement, the rating agency did not take note of many of the government's recent initiatives including fertilizer subsidy reform, capping subsidies as a fraction of Gross Domestic Product (GDP) and new manufacturing and telecom policies.

Two days after Finance Minister Pranab Mukherjee threw a hint in favour of a policy rate cut "for the sake of growth", Reserve Bank of India Governor D Subbarao surprised the market on 25th June, 2012 by keeping the repo rate and cash reserve ratio (CRR) unchanged at eight per cent and 4.75 per cent, respectively.

Central Bank put the onus of growth revival on finance ministry. It disappointed industry by keeping rates unchanged.

The mid-quarter review of monetary policy, in fact, went a step further by putting the onus of bringing growth on track on the government. "Our assessment of the current growth-inflation dynamic is that there are several factors responsible for the slowdown in activity, particularly in investment, with the role of interest rates being relatively small.

Mukherjee took care not to show his disappointment and said high inflation numbers might have weighed on the RBI's decision-making process. In any case, "it was not necessary for the governor to consult the minister in the mid-quarter review," he added.

The RBI said it would also look at the Consumer Price Index, which was in double digits. "Apart from a lack of fiscal consolidation, retail inflation and the absence of a pass-through of international crude oil prices, to domestic prices were the main reasons for growing inflationary expectations," the RBI said. The rupee depreciation had "significantly offset" the impact of falling global oil prices, it added.

The RBI increased banks' limit on export credit refinance from 15 per cent to 50 per cent. That has the potential to release additional liquidity of Rs 30,000 crore, equivalent to a 50-bp CRR cut. Bankers, however, said the step might not make any material difference as the existing limit had not been used fully.

Now talks about over promising and under-delivering. Pranab Mukherjee inflated the market's hopes that he'd taken bold measures to boost investor confidence, but came up with only few small tweaks on his last day as Finance Minister.

FDI in Insurance and Pension Sector

The proposal for 49 per cent FDI in insurance and pension sector was made during Pranab Mukherjee's tenure when he was the Finance Minister. However, the decision on the same was delayed because of resistance from the cronies.

In a move aimed at encouraging investment sentiment in the country, the Finance Ministry on 22 August, 2012 approved 49 per cent foreign direct investment in insurance and pension sector. Earlier the permitted level of FDI in the insurance and pension sector was 26 per cent.

With the approval of Union Finance Ministry, the bill is to be discussed in the Cabinet and will require to be approved by the Parliament.

As per the Insurance Regulatory and Development Authority (IRDA) estimates, over the next five years, the insurance sector requires a capital infusion of more than 12 billion dollar. The Union Government has been trying hard to introduce the major reforms to revive the ailing economy. Despite facing vehement opposition from different political parties, the measure such as FDI in multi-brand retail has been cleared by both the Houses of the Parliament eventually.

Indian economy is rapidly moving towards the grim economic situation similar faced during the recession. The economy needs some big ticket reforms to reverse the pessimistic economic environment. India's GDP growth fell to 6.5 per cent during 2011-12 but the fourth quarter growth rate dropped to 5.3 per cent, the slowest in past nine years. Business confidence among the investors and business leaders has touched the historic low as industrial output and trade figures are constantly going down.

The tight monetary policy measures adopted by the Central Bank to check inflation has actually aggravated the situation as high interest rates are hugely impacting the overall growth scenario. Indian industries have been reiterating that there is an urgent need to create conditions for revival of private investment.

The FDI in insurance might prove to be a start of the long pending reform but the Union Finance Minister P Chidambaram will have to work hard on political front to make it possible. Earlier the government had to defer the decision on the Bill as it faced opposition from its allies such as Trinamool Congress.

Black Money Stashed Abroad

Union Finance Minister Pranab Mukherjee said all the money kept by Indians abroad is not black money and noted that India has signed treaties with 37 countries to know the details of such illegal wealth.

He said "Not all money kept abroad is black money... It might have been deposited by businessmen or business houses. The process will take time to know the exact amount".

The government had earlier proposed a multi-faceted strategy to unearth black money through fast-track courts and deterrent punishment but had ruled out any tax immunity schemes.

The White Paper on black money tabled by Mukherjee in the Lok Sabha favoured a strategic mix of four pillars that will include incentives for voluntary compliance, reforms in vulnerable sectors of economy, creating effective credible deterrence and supportive measures.

The 97-page report however, did not give out any name of black money holders or estimated of such funds either in the country or outside but referred to estimates made earlier by various domestic and foreign institutions.

Last Day as FM

He may be 'embarking upon a new journey', but Pranab Mukherjee tried to stick to his regular schedule till his last day as the country's Finance Minister. Dressed in a crisp white cotton kurta and dhoti with a cream coloured waistcoat, the minister arrived at his North Block office around 12 pm after his customary morning walk, *puja* and breakfast.

But the first floor of North Block where the finance minister's office is located wore an unusually relaxed look and had an almost convivial atmosphere. Instead of officers walking in and out of Mukherjee's office, with stacks of files in their arms; seen was a long line of visitors armed with flowers and garlands who had come to bid farewell to the Finance Minister.

"Standing on the brink of such an honour, I also feel a tinge of sentiment at the thought of leaving behind my life as a political activist, spanning over four decades. I will miss my colleagues in the ministry of finance," he said minutes before he left to submit his resignation.

Keeping current tight situation in mind, the out-going Finance Minister Pranab Mukherjee took few authentic steps to curb the current deficit like RBI looking at steps to bring economy back on track.

The Political FM

Pranab Mukherjee always defends himself by claiming that Budgets are political documents. "We are not economists, technocrats or civil servants. I get the back-up from civil servants and economists, but I am a political activist. And my Budget is essentially a document that follows our political ideology," Mukherjee said.

In fact, captains of Indian industry patiently waited and watched for the first one and half years of UPA-II. They were disappointed when Mukherjee's July 2009 Budget, did not have any big-ticket announcement on reforms. The FM instead, hiked social sector outlays. India Inc didn't say much - at least not openly. After all, India' economy was still growing strongly.

Other Budget Speeches

The Parliament has so far hosted 80 Budget speeches, including interim and special-situation budgetary proposals

- The first union Budget of independent India was presented by the then Finance Minister RK Shanmukham Chetty, on November 26, 1947.
- The maximum number of 10 Budgets, have been presented by Morarji Desai, while Mukherjee will join the league of P Chidambaram, Yashwant Sinha, YB Chavan and CD Deshmukh, who have presented seven Budgets, each, in the past.
- Prime Minister Manmohan Singh and the country's fourth Finance Minister TT Krishnamachari have presented six Budgets each during their tenures in the Finance Ministry.
- Mukherjee has so far presented six annual Budgets, including the Budgets for two consecutive financial years, 2010-11 and 2011-12, and an interim Budget

before that for the fiscal year 2009-10. Way back in early 80s also, Mukherjee had presented three consecutive Budgets.

- Among others, R Venkatraman and HM Patel have presented three Budgets each, while Jaswant Singh, VP Singh, C Subramaniam, John Mathai and RK Shanmukham Chetty have two Budgets each to their credits.
- Besides, Jawaharlal Nehru, Indira Gandhi, Rajiv Gandhi, Charan Singh, ND Tiwari, Madhu Dandwate, SB Chavan and Sachindra Chaudhuri have presented one Budget each.

Chapter - VIII

Mediation in Lokpal Row

Committed To Strong Lokpal Bill

The rampant corruption in the country, which is severely hampering day-to-day necessities and requirements of the masses, has resulted in huge resentment against the functioning of the government. The Commonwealth Games and 2G scams raised the furor to a feverish pitch. The peoples' anger was channelized in a massive protest led by the social activist Anna Hazare, aided by civil society members who demanded setting up of an ombudsman -'Lokpal', to investigate corruption in the government. Though a bill for setting up the Lokpal was first thought of, almost 40 years ago, successive governments have avoided putting the bill in place.

Pushed to the wall, the Manmohan Singh government was forced to appoint a joint committee of group of ministers and civil society members. The committee, in charge of drafting it, was set up after a hunger strike in April 2011 by 72-year-old Gandhian Anna Hazare. He became the driving force in this people's movement that demanded the government prove its intent, to introduce a radical and tough new Bill, for a strong and autonomous Lokpal. The Lokpal

Bill Committee was set up to ensure Anna Hazare ended his hunger strike. It paired five ministers with five activists - Anna Hazare, Santosh Hegde, Arvind Kejriwal, Prashant Bhushan, and former Law Minister Shanti Bhushan, who was declared as the co-chair of the committee, at par with the Finance Minister.

Pleads For a Lokpal Bill

Finance Minister Pranab Mukherjee who was on the Lokpal Bill drafting committee for a brief period, promised that the working of that committee, "won't be affected by the controversies over some members. Committee's government members will work with Anna Hazare and colleagues, to draft a strong Lokpal bill".

Pranab Mukherjee wanted that the legislation on the Lokpal Bill must be done on the floor of the House. He initiated a debate on Lokpal Bill in Lok Sabha. He began by recounting the chain of events since Anna Hazare first went on fast at the Jantar Mantar on 9 April, 2011.

"There is nothing wrong in dialogue with civil society, but I also don't agree when they say it should be only their view," he added.

Accusing the political parties of taking contradictory stand on the Lokpal Bill issue, Mukherjee said: "Nothing has come from a magician's hat. Everything was discussed. The government received mandate at all-party meeting. Not under duress, not under threat. We wanted to have effective strong anti-corruption legislation in the form of Lokpal Bill. Quota was also brought up. The government draft is based on day long discussion in Parliament".

Participating in a debate on the Lokpal Bill in Lok Sabha, Bharatiya Janata Party (BJP) leader Yashwant Sinha said: "The way the Prime Minister listed his government's achievements seemed like an exit speech. The government wants to shove this bill down our throats. Why? You have deliberately created a weak and helpless Lokpal".

Yashwant Sinha further accused the government of deliberately creating a weak and helpless Lokpal.

"A morally bankrupt government has brought not a Lokpal Bill but a 'Brokepal' Bill. What this government has put us through with its scandals that is why an old man is on a fast. The honest PM heads the most corrupt government India has ever had. This is why people are restless and desperate for change," said Sinha.

"Prevention of Corruption Act covers everyone from peon to PM; so does Indian Penal Code. These two laws are what the Lokpal will enforce, isn't it? Not one minister from Atalji's Government is in any jail. Minority reservation - you (UPA Government) have introduced this, you know it will not stick," he added.

Responding to Sinha, Mukherjee said, "On August 27, we agreed on this through 'Sense of the House'. You say federal structure will be compromised. But we are going to bring amendment to provide that without consent of state governments, it will not be enacted. Forty years we have waited. I did not expect Yashwant Sinha to say this is (PM) a farewell speech".

"Why are you in a hurry? Why don't you wait for two years more? Prime Minister is not giving farewell speech. Prime Minister has introduced new direction in parliamentary democracy. He suggested engaging with civil society," he added.

Mukherjee countered the attack of Yashwant Sinha and further said, "Government followed established procedures in introducing Lokpal Bill in Parliament. Whatever we do, should be within the Constitution. We are at crossroads; let us try to find solution within constitutional framework, without violating supremacy of Parliament.

He asked the MPs to discuss whether:

- The jurisdiction of the proposed Lokpal should cover all employees of the central government. This is Hazare's key issue asking the government to include lower bureaucracy, which interacts with the common man and often harasses it, within the ambit of an independent and strong anti-graft watchdog.

- Lokpal will operate through the institution of the Lokayukta in all states. This is Hazare's second demand.
- Lokpal should have the power to punish all those who violate the "grievance redressal mechanism" to be put in place.

Hazare in his communications with the government had demanded that parliament pass a resolution agreeing in principle to set up Lokayuktas in states, frame Citizen's Charters for all government departments and include lower bureaucracy in the ambit of Lokpal.

"The specific issues raised by Hazare were important. They deserve our serious consideration. In case a consensus emerges at the end of the discussion, the Standing Committee will, in the course of their deliberations, take into account their practicability, implementability and constitutionality". He added, "whatever the House decides should be consistent with the principles enshrined within our constitutional framework," said Mukherjee.

Expressing concern over the health of Anna Hazare, Pranab Mukherjee requested him to end his fast. The government also hoped that Anna Hazare would end his fast soon.

After Mukherjee's statement in Lok Sabha on the Lokpal issue, the House was to discuss the matter further, including the Jan Lokpal Bill drafted by Team Anna.

Pranab slams BJP over Lokpal

Desperate to win back some lost ground on the demand for a Jan Lokpal Bill, the Congress put the onus on the Opposition to pass the legislation in Parliament.

Pranab Mukherjee, the Congress party's key political strategist and troubleshooter, threw an open challenge to the BJP saying, "it was up to the Opposition to ensure passage of the first people-drafted Bill in Parliament". Mukherjee said the government was even ready to pass the Bill in the monsoon session itself, without sending the draft Bill to the Parliament's standing committee - provided the BJP cooperated.

Pranab vs Advani: Responding to BJP leader LK Advani's demand that the Bill be passed in the next session of Parliament, Mukherjee said "Instead of making announcements from the platform, let him (Advani) ensure that his members in the Lok Sabha and the Rajya Sabha will co-operate with us".

The Congress hoped to put the BJP in a tight spot with this move, since the political class as a whole, including the BJP, is extremely wary of some of the tough provisions proposed to be included in the new anti-graft Bill especially those relating to elected representatives.

Samajwadi Party general secretary Mohan Singh, NCP general secretary Tariq Anwar and former Union minister and senior RLD leader Raghuvansh Prasad Singh had already expressed fears that the proposed law would undermine parliamentary democracy.

Jammu & Kashmir chief minister Omar Abdullah tweeted that people's power was not just "three nights of candles & music" and that he was "amused to see the sort of people trying to jump on the Hazare bandwagon".

The Congress's actual thinking on the 'people's Bill' was evident in AICC general secretary Digvijay Singh's cautious comments.

"We have to be a little careful that the Prime Minister or ministers duly elected by more than one billion people of the country are not in any way subjected to any form of whims of the people in the (drafting) committee on the Lokpal Bill," he said.

But by firmly putting the ball in the BJP's court for turning the Bill into law, the Congress hoped to achieve two things:

- First, limit damage to the party's image after Anna Hazare's movement led to an unprecedented mobilisation of the people against corruption.
- The second, to leverage the misgivings of the political class about the 'anti-politician' provisions in the proposed Bill in order to try and delay or scuttle the Bill.

It was a win-win situation for the Congress. While outright scuttling or watering down of the Bill would have suited the interest of all political parties, the BJP could have been made the villain of the piece for this.

In fact, the Congress was attempting to suggest that past attempts to introduce a tough anti-graft Bill had also been stymied by the BJP. Hitting back at Advani for dubbing the UPA government as the most corrupt, Mukherjee asked why the NDA had failed to get it enacted while they were in power.

"What had Advani done? What prevented him from getting the Lokpal Bill passed when he was the home minister while the NDA was in power?" Mukherjee thundered.

Advani, who was out on the campaign trail for the BJP, insisted that his party was keen to see the Bill through, "I got a call from Pranab Mukherjee, and I have assured him the full support of my party for it. The Bill should not just be presented in Parliament but also be passed," the BJP strongman said.

The Congress Party said that because of the anti-politicians mood in civil society after the Jantar Mantar agitation, many leaders were scared to speak out on the "draconian" Jan Lokpal Bill in public.

Party insiders said there are a number of chief ministers and former chief ministers who have been in the thick of corruption charges in BJP-ruled Karnataka, Uttarakhand, Chhattisgarh, Madhya Pradesh, the BSP-ruled Uttar Pradesh and the DMK ruled Tamil Nadu.

Former chief ministers like Mulayam Singh Yadav, Lalu Prasad and Jayalalithaa are still fighting graft cases against them. "All of them should go to jail if the new Bill is enacted," a senior AICC leader said.

Though some Opposition leaders made pulpit speeches supporting Hazare and the Jan Lokpal Bill, they are unlikely to support any legislation which has provisions weakening the "supremacy of Parliament", senior political leaders said off the record.

"The issue was good but their method was fascist. In a democracy, laws are enacted by Parliament and not NGOs. They are trying to imply that only NGOs are honest and that all politicians are corrupt," Samajwadi Party general secretary Mohan Singh said.

Even the Left parties were worried. Asked if the CPM would support such a Bill, a party leader said supporting the Bill would depend on "the kind of provisions" in it, signalling the unease in the political class.

CPM leaders will sit after the election campaign was over and take a call on the Bill, a party insider said, adding, "Our stand is clear, we will not support anything that undermines Parliament's supremacy".

He said concentration of vast powers in one single entity is not desirable. "Look at what Gorbachev did, he dismantled the Communist Party".

Two Amendments to Bill

Pranab Mukherjee as head of GOM on corruption suggested two amendments, the first amendment now allows only Members of Parliament (MPs) to move for removal of a member or the head of the Lokpal panel. The two clauses, which allowed the President or any citizen to move for their removal, have now been removed. According to the amendment, the move for removal can be made now only through a petition signed by not less than 100 MPs.

The other amendment is that the Lokpal Bill will be applicable to a state only upon passing a resolution by the state legislature. The Lokpal refers to a national ombudsman agency which will investigate complaints of graft against government servants. The bill in its earlier form made it necessary for states to create a Lokyukta, or local agency, that replicates the national model.

Lok Sabha Creates History

Dr Singh in his speech made in the Lok Sabha said: "There are some very special moments in the life of a nation. This is one such moment. The nation waits with bated breath how the collective wisdom of this House will be reflected in the vote at the end of the debate on the Lokpal and Lokayuktas Bill, 2011. The broad provisions of this Bill have been vigorously debated both in the public domain and by political parties.

"It is my honest belief that the Bill that is now before the House lives up to the promise that members of this House collectively made to the people of this country by way of the sense of the House at the end of the debate on 27th August, 2011. The task of legislation is very serious business and must eventually be performed by all of us who have been constitutionally assigned this duty. Others can persuade and have their voices heard. But the decision must rest with us," he added.

Emphasising, that the government held a wide range of consultations ahead of drafting the Lokpal Bill, Dr. Singh said: "At the same time we must keep in mind the fact that corruption and its consequences eat into the body politic. We have seen how public anger has manifested itself in the last one year. Let us, therefore, endorse this Bill as proposed. In drafting this legislation we have had a wide range of consultations".

"We have been enriched by the wisdom of political parties and all shades of opinion have been taken into account," he added.

The Prime Minister further said the Central Bureau of Investigation (CBI) should function without interference through any Government 'dictat', but no entity should be created which has 'onerous executive responsibilities without any accountability'.

Finance Minister Pranab Mukherjee had also echoed similar sentiments as the Prime Minister, and said that the legislation on the Lokpal Bill must be done on the floor of the House.

"The debate has been lively. Various points have been covered. The government has not moved in undue haste. For last six months, we are debating this issue inside the House. Country is agitating and debating this issue outside the House. They are the decision-makers, not suggestion-givers," said Mukherjee.

The much awaited Lokpal Bill was passed in the Lok Sabha after certain amendments, in Deccember 2011. The anti-graft Bill was passed by voice vote even as the leaders of the Bharatiya Janata Party (BJP), Left and the Samajwadi Party walked out of the House.

The Bill however got stuck in the Rajya Sabha, as opposition parties suggested more than 150 amendments, which was impossible for the government to debate and incorporate in the Bill during the short Rajya Sabha session.

Chapter - IX

Adieu to Active Politics

On being nominated as Presidential candidate as per convention the candidates are supposed to be resigning from their respective political party, as, President of India is required to be apolitical and politically neutral. Pranab Mukherjee accordingly resigned from the Congress party and cabinet on 26th June, 2012.

PM writes emotional letter to Pranab

Prime Minister Manmohan Singh, in a rare gesture, wrote a personal letter to Pranab Mukherjee after Dada resigned from the Union Cabinet as finance minister on 26th June, 2012. Perhaps in a bid to scotch rumours about the lack of chemistry between him and Mukherjee, the PM showered praise on Dada, the UPA's presidential candidate.

"Our government owes a deep debt of gratitude to you for your invaluable contribution to its work over the last eight years," Singh said.

The PM said he hoped to see Mukherjee occupy the position of President next month. "I also wish you sustained good health and happiness in the years to come," the PM said, adding that he has forwarded Mukherjee's resignation to the President. "I have benefited from your wise counsel on innumerable occasions and we will all deeply miss your presence amidst us". the letter further added.

Gets Touching Farewell

There were no tears, but it was an emotional farewell as presidential nominee Pranab Mukherjee on 25th June, 2012 bid adieu to the Congress Working Committee (CWC), the highest decision-making body of the party after 34 years of distinguished service.

A special CWC meeting was convened at Congress president Sonia Gandhi's official residence at 10 Janpath to give him a warm farewell. Mukherjee was expected to wind up all pending work by 26th June 2012 afternoon, before demitting office as finance minister. Senior Congress leaders, led by Sonia Gandhi and Prime Minister Manmohan Singh, lavished praises on Finance Minister Pranab Mukherjee at this special Congress Working Committee meeting.

Singh said he will miss Mukherjee in the government, but will be happy to see him as President. He added that Mukherjee had a very heavy responsibility in the government. Sonia hailed Mukherjee as the senior most member of the CWC and said it was a matter of great pleasure that the UPA made him a presidential candidate. She expressed her gratitude to all those parties in the UPA and outside for their support to Mukherjee. She added that Mukherjee is getting the kind of support because of his "virtues".

An emotional Mukherjee said: "I got more from my party than what I contributed to it in my entire life". He added that he always considered himself a true Congressman and did whatever was good for the party. He recalled his long association with the CWC and thanked the party for nominating him for the President's post".

"Soon I will not be a political entity," Pranab Mukherjee remarked hours before he resigned as finance minister to contest Presidential poll, but promised the 'quote seeking' media to deliver his "last message" before he bids adieu.

Pranab Mukherjee received a warm send off from officials of Finance Ministry whom he thanked for the support extended during his three-year stint at North Block.

"I got full support of all officials in whatever I achieved so far as a finance minister. I thank all the officials for their support and co-operation," he remarked at a send-off hosted by officials including finance secretary RS Gujral, economic affairs secretary R Gopalan and chief economic advisor Kaushik Basu.

No Regrets

Pranab Mukherjee expresses no sign of unhappiness on missing out, being the prime minister of the country. His cheerful disposition and gentle smile does not give away any feeling of regret. Regret, if any, may lie buried or embedded, somewhere deep in the corner of his heart, but then again, maybe there isn't any. It is only perceived that there is regret, by people who do not know him, and his magnanimity.

Commending Manmohan Singh as the best man for the job, Pranab said "I don't regret not being the Prime Minister. Manmohan Singh is worthy of being PM. He will be the second man who'll complete two terms".

Did Manmohan, Pranab share uneasy equations?

In a rare gesture, Prime Minister Manmohan Singh was one of the two proposers for Mukherjee at the time of his filing of nomination papers on 28th June, 2012, to add a personal touch to the Congress veteran's candidacy.

PMO sources said that this step had been taken to give the signal that Mukherjee was the PM's candidate and both the party and the government were on the same page on his nomination.

But despite the bonhomie, a gulf had opened up between the prime minister and his deputy over the direction of economic policies over the past year, notably over a controversial proposal enabling the government to retrospectively tax overseas deals involving Indian assets.

The amendment, which many regard as overturning a Supreme Court ruling that had said Vodafone would not have to pay tax on the purchase of its Indian telecom business, did not find favour with the PMO. The move which has attracted widespread international opprobrium, also appeared to contradict Singh's assurance to Gordon Brown, Britain's prime minister in 2009, that Vodafone would be able to contest tax claims before the Indian judiciary. Though Mukherjee rolled back many measures proposed in the 2012 Budget, he stuck to his guns on Vodafone.

People in the know of goings on in the corridors of power say that, the prime minister has also been less than impressed by the finance ministry's response to threats of downgrades by rating agencies and to the continuing slide of the rupee.

There were also differences between Singh, and Mukherjee in 2011 on granting a fresh two-year term to RBI Governor Duvvuri Subbarao. Singh, himself a former central bank chief, eventually prevailed, resulting in Subbarao heading the central bank for a second term.

A former secretary in the finance ministry who has worked with Singh and a string of finance ministers says, "There has been a role reversal compared to the past when you had a politically strong prime minister and a competent finance minister. In this case, Mukherjee has a strong political standing of his own and was often called to douse a lot of fires. That would have meant the prime minister going soft even when it was evident that economic management was faltering".

Yashwant Sinha, BJP leader and former finance minister, says the relationship was a troubled one and it did reflect in economic management. "No finance minister, however powerful he is, will be out on a limb without the complete and unflinching support of the prime minister, who has to play the role of a friend, philosopher and guide when it comes to day-to-day issues," he says.

Fate has now offered Pranab a much grander office in Rashtrapati Bhavan. On his way to hand in his resignation to the Prime Minister on June 26 2012, he told mediapersons outside North Block, "Today, I stand ready to embark on a new journey". As the media thronged him for that last sound bite, he happily obliged: "This is what I will miss. Not being stopped by all of you while getting into my car outside the Ministry of Finance". Then he added, "Sometimes, I have even snubbed you but you have always cooperated".

This is precisely what the Congress and UPA will miss: A leader with the stature to snub without offending. Mukherjee's promotion has left a vacuum, both in Government and the party.

Midas Touch

If there is one politician in India, who has earned the right to occupy the highest office through years of distinguished service, it is the 77-year-old Mukherjee. The stalwart from Bengal, will certainly lift the institution of the presidency to great heights.

Rashtrapati Bhavan's gain will be a loss for the Congress party and the UPA Government. For them, the former finance minister and future president was a man for all seasons. For a party, whose president, Mrs Sonia Gandhi, joined active politics only as recently as 1998 and whose prime minister joined politics only a little earlier in 1991, Mukherjee's long political experience was a real asset. He joined politics in 1966 and first became a minister in 1973. He rose quickly to become Indira Gandhi's right-hand man and was finance minister at the young age of 47 in 1982. There is no one in the Congress with such a vast experience, who can fill the void left behind by departure of Pranab Mukherjee from the party.

There is more to Mukherjee than his experience. It is a great folly to believe that government is best run by technocrats, and not politicians. Managing a government requires the political skill of the highest order. Mukherjee was a rare political statesman, a real heavyweight, in a party that is now increasingly dominated by armchair politicians. His sharp political instincts made him a vital asset in an era of fractured, coalition politics. He was the party's and government's bridge with allies. Manmohan Singh may claim all the credit for the nuclear deal, but it was Mukherjee's political manoeuvres which ensured that the deal went through in the parliament and the Government stayed alive.

Mukherjee was the troubleshooter with civil society, represented by Team Anna, when all the other leading lights of the Congress, who are now shadow-boxing to take Mukherjee's place, had failed miserably. In an indecisive Government, the former finance minister was one who could take decisions. It's no wonder that he chaired 13 of the Government's 14 Empowered Group of Ministers (EGoMs) when he quit office.

The finance ministry certainly needs revival. Mukherjee's Midas touch deserted him in his last stint in North Block. The slumping economy is not his fault alone. A finance minister cannot alone break the logjam and paralysis across the Government. The economy has to emerge from its paralytic pessimism and UPA 2 from its political miasma.

Not all my decisions right

On the last day of his 43 years in active politics, outgoing finance minister Pranab Mukherjee, 77, turned emotional as he admitted that he may have made some mistakes as a policy-maker. In the backdrop of sharp criticism from some quarters over his performance as finance minister, Mukherjee said, "Not every decision I have taken might have been right. But I took them keeping in view the interest of the people whose faces appeared before me more often than not".

His tenure as finance minister also coincided with the world economic crisis in 2008 and again the renewed prospects of a slowdown in 2012.

Pranab Mukherjee, who received both bouquet and brickbats for his decisions, said criticism and appreciation, reminded him of his duties.

"Members of the media, friends like you, have always reminded me of my responsibilities, most of the time, through your criticism, sometimes through your appreciation, what I should do as a representative of the people," he said.

"I hope these duties you will continue so long I am in public life," he said.

The man used to being in the hot seat has already charted out his plans after retiring from politics. "After retiring from politics, I wanted to read books. (The) Library would be my destination".

A LONG JOURNEY: The Bird's Eye View

Pranab Mukherjee is a rare politician, who has never been a mass leader, but commands the attention of the nation, like very few in his tribe can. It is a quality that is expected to stand him in good stead, as he makes it to the Rashtrapati Bhavan, presidential mansion sitting majestically atop Raisina Hills.

Quintessential Congressman

All through his political career, he has been successful in maintaining an unblemished image, and upholding probity, in public life. He devours books, works almost 16 hours a day, well past midnight, and said, in a rare peek into his personal life, in an interview some years ago, he hardly found time for his family. His only interaction was often limited to giving his wife a goodnight peck before retiring to bed, well past the usual bedtime.

His Congress colleagues, whisper he is a '*Chanakya*,' ancient India's fabled political philosopher, but he is largely well liked for his knowledge and sagacity. "No one in the party is against him, he has no enemies," said a Congress minister.

Though Pranab was the quintessential number two in the Congress-led government, the 77-year-old Mukherjee is a man of unparalleled experience who has the rare distinction of having served at different times as Foreign, Defence and Finance minister, respectively. For the last 25 years, he has presided over Cabinet meetings, when the Prime Minister has been away.

Troubleshooter

From the time he was first appointed a minister for revenue and banking by Indira Gandhi in 1973, Mukherjee has held a variety of portfolios in successive governments.

But once he returned to the government, particularly under Manmohan Singh, he emerged with his prodigious bank of knowledge, and varied political experience, as the principal troubleshooter and consensus-creator in the government.

He was the man in the Congress - both Sonia Gandhi and Manmohan Singh - have turned to him every time there was a political crisis. According to Rabi Banerjee who wrote in '*The Week*' magazine (August 5, 2012) , "In Pranab Mukherjee's going, the Congress and West Bengal have lost a bridge, one that they used quite often to get across troubled waters. When allies play rough, the Congress cannot now look to the lone ranger from Jangipur to pull out his six- shooters and restore order". Whenever required, Mukherjee has risen to the occasion, and even if he has not always succeeded, he invariably left a mark in parliamentary debates.

Indispensability

His indispensability is reflected in the number of key ministerial decision-making groups, known as Group of Ministers, he has been asked to head since 2004 -- of the 183 groups formed, 83 were under him.

He is considered a walking encyclopedia on virtually everything related to politics and governance, which makes it difficult for any bureaucrat to hoodwink or trip him.

A former secretary in the government, who worked under him when Mukherjee was Foreign Minister remarked,

"He has a photographic memory for the fine print, and remembers negotiating details and their articles and clauses, like nobody can. So whatever you tell him, he will tell you more about it".

His sharp memory, quick wit and persuasive skills are widely respected. In what can be called a tribute, BJP stalwart LK Advani once remarked, that the Congress-led UPA government would not last a day, but for, Pranab Mukherjee.

He is down to earth, lives modestly and has admitted, many a time that he cannot speak polished English. For one who is supremely self-confident, he can be humble. But he has a temper, and has more than once, apologised to MPs, for raising his voice.

Congress' Deft Manager

Pranab was the man, who played a remarkable role in the huge transformation of India's socialist economy to the post-globalisation market economy in the 90s. Since, his foray in politics, Pranab has emerged as the man of all seasons for his party, and therefore, held key positions in the government and the Party.

He was a powerful Minister of State for Revenue during Emergency and in nine years from 1973, he rose to become the Finance Minister in Indira Gandhi's Cabinet.

Mukherjee was AICC general secretary in 1998-99. In 1984-1991, 1996 and 1998, Mukherjee was Chairman of the Campaign Committee of AICC for Conducting National Election to Parliament, besides being a member in the Congress Working Committee, and Congress Election Committee.

He also headed the Congress Parliamentary Party and the Congress Legislative Party which consists of all the Congress MPs and MLAs in the country. This is apart from being Leader of the House in Lok Sabha, Bengal Pradesh Congress Committee President.

Pranab–Manmohan: The Chasers

When Pranab was Finance Minister of the country, Manmohan Singh was appointed RBI Governor in 1982. In what could be described a case of chasing each other's shadow, Manmohan Singh became Deputy Chairman of Planning Commission from 1985 to 1987, a post Pranab Mukherjee later held from 1991 to 1996, when Manmohan Singh became Finance Minister under PV Narsimha Rao government.

Pranab Mukherjee also had a brief stint as Chairman of the Economic Advisory Cell of AICC between 1987 and 1989. Interestingly, Manmohan Singh also held this post, when Congress was out of power between 1999 and 2004.

Despite his track record and senior status in the party and the Government, Sonia Gandhi's preferred Manmohan as Prime Minister when the UPA-1 came to power in 2004. Yet the mutual respect Pranab and Manmohan shared for each other is indicated by an incident, when Pranab Mukherjee once threatened not to attend Core Committee Meetings after the Prime Minister Manmohan Singh referred to him as 'Sir'. The two reached an arrangement: Singh calls him 'Pranab Ji" and Pranab reciprocate by saying "Dr Singh".

Pranab: Congress Man of all Times

Ever seen as the perennial 'No 2' in the Congress, on whose ticket he became a Rajya Sabha member, Mukherjee may have missed becoming the Prime Minister on a couple of occasions, but still, he was the man to whom the government looked to, during times of crisis.

It is no surprise that sparing him from the government, to be nominated as presidential candidate was a huge dilemma for the Congress President Sonia Gandhi, who trusted him as a deft manager of the government that has often moved from crisis to crisis in both the versions of UPA 1 and UPA 2.

Mukherjee was also jocularly called 'GoM Mukherjee' in political circles as he headed close to 83 Group of Ministers on various key issues including the recent one on setting up of the 'Lokpal.'

Chapter - X

Cardinal Richelieu

Mukherjee, a veteran of four decades in politics, has been called the Congress party's chief trouble-shooter, crisis manager and even a modern-day Cardinal Richelieu, the clergyman who was the powerful right-hand man to French King Louis XIII.

When his name first surfaced as a potential candidate for the presidency, a Congress spokeswoman said he was too indispensable to the party, but media reports suggested Sonia was uneasy about installing a man in the presidential palace who was unlikely to prove as compliant as his predecessors.

Mukherjee is lauded for his ability to reach across party lines, but critics say, as finance minister he has been too complacent, failing to rein in spending on fuel, food and fertilizer subsidies, and win across party support, for reforms to boost flagging economic growth.

Since delivering his latest budget in March 2012 he was also criticized for his tough stand on tax proposals that scared off foreign investors, and insistence that the euro zone crisis is largely to blame for the economy's woes. Economists say policy inertia at home is also a major factor.

It is common knowledge that Mukherjee has grown tired of the day-to-day politics of a divided coalition government that has failed to implement any major economic reforms since coming to power in 2004.

It was close to midnight, before the results of the presidential elections were declared; Mukherjee, seated behind a desk piled with files, was tearing open envelopes and reading them as he responded to questions from correspondents. On a wall behind him was a sepia-coloured picture of his mentor, Indira Gandhi. Mukherjee was characteristically circumspect about his ambitions and the role of the new president, but his answers hinted at a more proactive approach were he to get the job.

"The president will have to apply his mind according to the Constitution. He has the right to be informed and be advised by the government," he said.

Why Sonia Nominated Pranab

In all probability, ruling Congress Party leader Sonia Gandhi nominated Pranab to become the next President of India, keeping in view that her party will face a tough parliamentary election in 2014, and he might just prove to be her trump card, in the event of a hung Parliament.

Until now, India's President has been viewed as a ceremonial head of state. But with the next elections widely expected to produce a fragmented parliament with no clear winner, Mukherjee, a loyal Congress man, will play a key role in deciding which party gets invited, to form the new government. Perhaps more importantly, Mukherjee could help the Gandhi family keep its grip on power.

Mukherjee was nominated by the Congress party in the face of mild opposition from a key ally, Mamata Banerjee's Trinamool Congress (TMC) within the ruling coalition. The party, however, won support from other coalition partners for its choice and was confident that Mukherjee would garner the Electoral College vote on July 19, 2012.

Turbulent Periods Ahead

Analysts say, Mukherjee could play an influential role in steering the country, through potentially, one of the most politically turbulent periods in modern Indian history.

With neither of the two main parties - Congress and the Bharatiya Janata Party - expected to win convincing majority in 2014, a fragile coalition that includes several regional parties could emerge to claim power. In that scenario, Mukherjee, famed for his political acumen, could as president, exercise more authority; taking advantage of a vaguely worded Constitution.

Wikileaks On Pranab's Ambition

A confidential cable from the US Embassy in New Delhi to Washington on October 24, 2006, revealed by Wikileaks, described Pranab as "extremely ambitious" and said Sonia and other Congress leaders "remain suspicious of him and do not want to provide him with an opportunity to push (Prime Minister) Manmohan Singh aside".

Wikileaks cables of US Embassy further reveals that he was passed over for the premiership in 2004 by Sonia in favour of Manmohan Singh, and also lost out the post of home minister, one of the most senior cabinet jobs. Sonia feared he might use it as a platform to campaign against the politically weaker and unelected Manmohan Singh.

Undeterred By Advancing Age

Pranab still has the spirit of youth. His advancing age has not deterred his monumental composure and spirit. Age has dimmed neither his ambitions nor his stamina. He still gets up at 6.00 am and does not go to bed until 2:00 am.

Miraculously Saved

Pranab was saved miraculously in April 2007 at the age of 72, when he held the post of foreign minister. His official car crashed head-on with a truck on the highway in West

Bengal. Mukherjee sustained head injuries that required stitches, but was back at work within days.

Mr Mukherjee was travelling from Murshidabad to Kolkata, when his car was hit by an oncoming truck, and skidded off the road after one of the tyres burst. The pilot car and other vehicles had moved on ahead. The condition of the driver and security guard were reported to be serious. The senior Congress leader was administered first aid and received 12 stitches at a hospital in Nakashipara in Bengal.

He was airlifted from Kolkata to Delhi, on a special plane and admitted to the Army's Research and Referral Hospital and a medical bulletin issued by doctors at the hospital said the 72-year-old Congress leader is "stable and cheerful". He received a head injury as well as other minor injuries during the accident.

Cautious Man

'Pranabda,' is a cautious man today as he has seen too many slips between the cup and the lip as he straddled along as the second in command for over four decades. "There is a long way to go. We are all aware of the situation and the numbers at play. The cards will be revealed in due course," he had said a few weeks before the Presidential elections.

Nobody is Indispensable

Mukherjee, when confronted with the obvious question as to how the government or the Congress party would survive without him, had said "Nobody is indispensable in life or politics. India survived after Nehru, Mrs Gandhi and Rajiv". While the country will wait and watch how Pranab Mukherje will fare as the 13th President of the country, what is certain, however, is that finding a replacement to this man will not be an easy job.

Deserving

Pranab Mukherjee certainly deserves the highest constitutional post in India and will prove to be the leader India needs, at this critical juncture.

It will be not easy for him, since the tasks and responsibilities he inherits, are huge. He would need to bring in political stability, lend a healing touch, allow room for harmonious coexistence, and to see that economical reforms get implemented. His clean image will ease his task, as he is modest in his approach and capable of dealing with both friends and foes. Being a true believer in democratic norms, a god- fearing .and a devoted family man, and being well versed in nuances of governance, makes him the ideal choice for the post. Pranab Mukherjee is open minded, a good listener and ready to apply his mind and heart whenever needed. He will be able to provide sound and objective advice to the political leadership of the country, as and when required.

Mukherjee, no doubt belongs to the old guard, but his ability to learn quickly and understand the needs, and apply the correctives, will make him more popular among the youth too. This is a rare combination for a leader in contemporary history.

As the chosen one for the job now, he is even more enthusiastic to leave an indelible impression in Indian history. He will be remembered for years to come, if he is allowed to function smoothly and without any roadblocks.

Famous for Temperament and ambience

Pranab Mukherjee - hails from a far-flung village of eastern India. But ever since he stepped into the national politics, he never looked back. He has been one of the principal characters of our national politics for four decades now— unmoved and unperturbed by the wins and losses as well as ups and downs of life.

Some might argue that he deserved much more in terms of rewards, recognition and responsibilities. They possibly tend to forget that he is beyond all these, in his own right. He has almost become a living legend by virtue of his scholastic genius, professional efficiency, indispensability and unparalleled acceptability among one and all.

Everybody always found Pranab da to be a person with greatly amiable temperament and a friendly disposition. Those who are in parliamentary politics have come to know and respect him, particularly over the past few years. Arun Jaitley Leader of the Opposition in the Rajya Sabha said to Pranab Mukherjee in the parliament on 18th October, 2011 that, "Many leaders in the government are smug and arrogant but you can charm even your critics". They all know him as an established leader of the House and an extremely efficient and competent minister. His remarkable equanimity in crisis situation is well known. Despite his humble beginnings he is someone, who has reached this high in life because of his own unquestionable merits. Right there on top, he is, because of his political and administrative acumen. He has all along been loyal to his ideology of putting nation before self, first and always.

Out of the 77 years of his life, he has spent no less than 42 years in the corridors of power, that too in the national Capital. Personally, he prefers being out of public glitter and glare. All through, he has been averse to publicity. For him, everything is just a part of life; everyday is just another day.

Behind every successful man there is a woman, so goes the maxim. His wife, Subhra Mukherjee's continuous support and appreciation for her husband as a man and his work, has played exactly that role.

Chapter - XI

Wranglings before Nomination

Law of Nature – 'A Vacuum is always Filled'

Veteran Congress leader Pranab Mukherjee's indispensability to the party nearly cost him the presidency. He said Sonia had told him he could not be spared as he still had much to do. Until Trinamool chief Mamata Banerjee's meeting with Congress president Sonia Gandhi on June 12th, Mukherjee was clubbed along with Vice President Hamid Ansari for the post of President. Describing how he emerged as the frontrunner, Mukherjee said Sonia initiated the discussion. "First she started talking to friendly parties that are part of the UPA government and discussed in general terms without mentioning any name. Then she discussed with the parties giving outside support to the UPA. After that she had discussions with important Congress leaders and in that course, names were thrown to her," he said. Until that stage, he said he wasn't in the picture.

Sonia told Mukherjee details of her June 12th meeting with Mamata. "That night she (Sonia) telephoned me and told me what exactly transpired. Thereafter, the next day, I had detailed discussions with her," said Mukherjee.

But, Mukherjee doesn't think he is indispensable. "In the law of nature, a vacuum is always filled". Even as the Congress is scouting for an able hand to replace Mukherjee to deal with crisis management, both at the Centre and in the party, the veteran leader feels there is no dearth of talent in the party to fill his shoes.

Speaking on coalitions, Mukherjee said, "My assessment is that it's not that the Indian people are asking for a coalition. The electorate is not finding a strong party that should be supported across the states, particularly in major states. "Once political parties, the Congress or some others, achieve that status, then they will have this advantage. But coalitions become necessary because a country like India cannot go on holding elections frequently. Remember how people started talking since 1984 when no party had emerged with decisive majority".

"But in 2009 I told that Congress might do better. Everybody wrote us off, when the Left party had separated from us. Therefore, it was quite natural for the people to believe that the Congress would be losing. What I am talking about is that the Indian democracy has the flexibility to accommodate and absorb difficult situations" Pranab says.

Candidates in the Fray for Nomination

Various persons were suggested by the Indian media and politicians, prior to official candidacies being submitted.

- Manmohan Singh, Prime Minister
- Pranab Mukherjee, Finance Minister
- Hamid Ansari, Vice President
- APJ Abdul Kalam, former President
- Gopal Krishna Gandhi, former Governor of Bengal and grandson of Mohandas Karamchand Gandhi
- Meira Kumar, Speaker of the Lok Sabha
- Somnath Chatterjee, former Speaker of the Lok Sabha
- AK Antony, Defence Minister

- Dr Karan Singh, Member of Rajya Sabha
- SY Quraishi, former Chief Election Commissioner
- Parkash Singh Badal, Chief Minister of Punjab
- Mulayam Singh Yadav, Samajwadi Party leader
- Mohsina Kidwai, Member of Rajya Sabha

With his candidature for the President's post gaining momentum, Pranab Mukherjee said to reporters at his residence "It is decided by the party. Party nominates. No one can become President on his own wish".

Incidentally Mukherjee's name was first revealed as UPA nominee publicly on 13th June by the West Bengal CM Mamata Banerjee after her meeting with Sonia Gandhi. However, within hours Mamata Banerjee, in the company of Mulayam Singh Yadav, addressed the media and surprised all by announcing former President APJ Abdul Kalam name. She expressed her support for Kalam on Facebook, the page for which garnered a large following. But soon after Sonia announced Mukherjee's name, SP changed their stance and came out in support of UPA's candidate, and Kalam remained solely Banerjee's choice. Initially, the BJP, Mohan Bhagawat, the Sarsanghchalak of the Rashtriya Swayamsevak Sangh, and Swami Rambhadracharya, a Hindu religious leader and author, also supported the candidacy of Kalam.

Kalam however let it be known that he may not contest the election if there was a chance he could lose the presidential election. On 18th June, Kalam said he would not run in the race following statement from JDU leader Nitish Kumar and SP leader Mulayam Singh Yadav that they would prefer to support Mukherjee. Following Kalam's decision, the BJP-led NDA turned to supporting PA Sangma.

UPA sources had said that Congress president Sonia Gandhi, who has been authorised by the party's working committee to pick the candidate, was likely to make the announcement around 15th June, 2012, probably a couple of days after the expected poll notification by the Election Commissioner.

The sources said the Congress has already secured the support of key allies like DMK, NCP and RLD, who form part of the government, and outside supporters like Samajwadi Party. BSP, another outside supporter and Trinamool Congress, UPA's second largest constituent, is not expected to oppose the UPA candidate.

Sangma' Candidature

The Nationalist Congress Party (NCP) chief Sharad Pawar announced his support for Mukherjee after talking with Sonia Gandhi. This made clear that there was no support for the former Lok Sabha speaker PA Sangma's candidature from within his own party. Sangma, however, said that he could still contest, though Sangma had said that he would not contest the election and instead support Kalam. He later decided to stay in the race despite the threat of sanctions from his party after a renewed pledge of support from the BJD's Naveen Patnaik. On 20th June, he resigned from the NCP following threats from his party.

Minister for Heavy Industries Praful Patel said: "We have supported Pranab Mukherjee who is the best choice for the country for the top constitutional post. Sangma should respect the party's decision and should not contest the elections. Sangma did not consult the party or senior leaders before announcing his candidature for the post. If he contests the election, it would violate party directive and invite action".

Sangma's daughter and MP Agatha Sangma campaigned for her father even though she was still a member of the NCP after her father left. As Minister for Rural Development, she told a meeting of tribals in the Bastar area of Chhattisgarh on 25th June that it would be a "welcome gesture" for tribal MPs and MLAs to vote for her father. This was then accompanied by the party's youth wing calling for her expulsion from the party. Her father later said that she would vote according to her "conscience".

Pranab Is UPA Candidate

Sonia Gandhi, while reading out from a statement announcing nomination of Mukherjee as UPA's presidential candidate, mentioned that Mukherjee possessed a long and distinguished record of public service, spanning over five decades. She said, "There is broad support for his candidature. The UPA appeals to all the political parties and all MPs and MLAs to support the candidature of Mukherjee for the office of president".

Thereafter, Prime Minister Manmohan Singh called up the senior BJP leader LK Advani, its president Nitin Gadkari and the leader of the opposition in the Lok Sabha Sushma Swaraj, apprising them of the decision to nominate Mukherjee.

Reacting to the nomination, the BJP spokesperson Shahnawaz Hussain said that, "it would have been better if the name was announced after due consultation with the opposition parties. The BJP would discuss with allies before taking a decision to support or oppose UPA candidate".

Friday 15th June 2012 Changed Pranab's Fate

On Friday, 15 June 2012, Sonia declared Mukherjee's name as the UPA candidate for the presidential polls. Sonia made the announcement during the crucial UPA meet held at Prime Minister Manmohan Singh's Race Course Road residence. In a statement issued by the party, it was highlighted that Pranab has a long and distinguished record and a broad support for his candidature. Soon after Sonia's announcement, the SP came out in support of Mukherjee's name. SP's General Secretary Ram Gopal Yadav said: "He is very happy that Pranabda has been finally nominated as the candidate for the biggest office. The party supports him and wishes him well for the victory".

In an unlikely move, even Bahujan Samaj Party president Mayawati came out in support of Mukherjee as presidential candidate. While addressing a press conference in Lucknow, she mentioned, "Among all the names that have been proposed for the post of President, Pranab Mukherjee is the most suitable and serious candidate. Congress President Sonia Gandhi spoke to me about his candidature and my party will support his name".

With support of the Samajwadi Party and the BSP assured, the UPA was comfortably placed to sail through the presidential election smoothly.

Even the Left came out and congratulated Mukherjee, but asserted that their stand on this issue would be decided during an internal meeting. Communist Party of India-Marxist (CPI-M) leader Brinda Karat said: 'We congratulate Pranab Mukherjee for the nomination but we shall decide our stand, post meeting"..

Events on the Decisive June 15th

- 11 am: The BJP-led NDA meet begins, senior leaders Sushma Swaraj, Jaswant Singh, Subramanian Swamy attended it at LK Advani's residence.
- 11.35 am: Mamata Banerjee addresses the media outside her residence. Says SP chief Mulayam Singh Yadav and she are still together and Kalam is their choice. She also appeals to all political parties to support Kalam.
- 12.05 pm: NCP Leader PA Sangma confirms, he is still in the presidential race and claims NDA's support.
- 12.15 pm: No consensus in NDA on Kalam; BJP and JD(U) differ on Kalam.
- 12.20 pm: Mamata skips UPA meet at 7, Race Course Road, leaves for Kolkata.
- 2:55 pm: Bihar Chief Minister and JD(U) leader Nitish Kumar meets Kalam in Patna.
- 3.00 pm: NDA meet, indecisive due to differences over supporting Kalam; Janata Dal (United) Sharad Yadav objects to supporting Kalam.

- 4 pm: Congress President Sonia Gandhi and Pranab Mukherjee reach Manmohan Singh's residence to attend UPA meet.
- 4:47 pm: Sonia announces Pranab Mukherjee as UPA nominee.
- 4:56 pm: Sonia appeals to all political parties to support Pranab.
- 5:18 pm: "Trinamool Congress is not going to change its stand on Pranab" says Kunal Ghosh, TMC, MP.
- 5:20 pm: Samajwadi Party announces its support for Pranab.
- 5.25 pm: The Left congratulates Pranab, but says party's stand will be decided during their meeting.
- 5.30 pm: The BJP says, though it was not consulted by the UPA before they declared their candidate, it will meet allies and decide on supporting Pranab Mukherjee.
- 5.35 pm: RJD chief Lalu Prasad Yadav backs Pranab as the Presidential candidate, reiterating he always said he would go with Sonia's choice.
- 5.38 pm: Addressing a press conference in Lucknow, Mayawati announces her support for Pranab.
- 5.51 pm: Manmohan Singh speaks to AB Bardhan, Mayawati, Mulayam Singh Yadav, Sushma Swaraj and Arun Jaitley.
- 6.12 pm: Pranab says he is deeply honoured to be nominated as the Presidential candidate and thanks Sonia; he says they have requested all political parties for their support, expressing confidence in his party members.
- 6.38 pm: Mulayam Singh says the three names he gave along with Trinamool Congress supremo Mamata Banerjee were only suggestions; declares his support for Pranab, calling him a man of high stature.

- 6.46 pm: DMK chief M Karunanidhi writes to Sonia expressing happiness at the selection of Pranab.
- 7.35 pm: Pranab Mukherjee appeals to all political parties to support his candidature for the Presidential poll.
- 8.45 pm: After her meeting with close aides, Mamata says she will speak on the Presidential poll on 16th June 2012.

President Bid a Victory for Tribals: Sangma

Opposition presidential candidate PA Sangma filed his nomination papers, flanked by BJP seniors LK Advani, Arun Jaitley, Sushma Swaraj, Ananth Kumar, Nitin Gadkari, BJD chief Naveen Patnaik, SAD's Parkash Singh Badal and Goa CM Manohar Parrikar, among others. Spelling out the campaign line, Sangma said, "Today is a victory of tribal unity... that a tribal is filing his nomination for the post of president".

"I have appealed to all political parties not to bring the campaign to the level of ordinary elections because presidential election has its own significance and stature," Mukherjee said in an apparent reference to Sangma playing the tribal card.

In another apparent reference to Sangma saying whips by political parties carry no weight in Presidential elections, Mukherjee said it was expected that members of parties would go by their parties' decisions.

"Please remember that in this election, members of the Electoral College, almost 99 per cent are of party nominees (legislators), besides the independents," he said.

"So, with (political) parties taking a decision, it is expected that the members will go along party lines," Mukherjee said.

Stating that there was nothing wrong in campaigning, the veteran leader said "But you have to keep this (not bringing the campaign down to ordinary level) in mind".

Nomination To Blunt Opposition Assault

The nomination of the Pranab Mukherjee, as the UPA candidate for the Rashtrapati Bhawan is probably a correct and decisive political decision since a long time, which the beleaguered UPA conglomeration has taken in its second tenure. The West Bengal politician – it goes without saying – is a formidable name and the opposition will find it difficult to oppose his candidature as bitterly as they did in the case of the outgoing president Pratibha Devisingh Patil.

After all, the senior BJP leader LK Advani, in 2009, had proferred encomiums on Mukherjee on the floor of the Lok Sabha, wondering how the UPA government would have functioned without the services of the veteran politician. Mukherjee's talent, acumen, expertise, zeal and tact have been repeatedly put to test, to defend the survival of the government headed by a person, who contributes the least to its running.

Personally for Mukherjee, the nomination comes as the high point of his career, as it also consigns to dustbin of history, the incident of October 1984, which for long made him a suspect in his loyalty, to the Congress' first family. However, some would point to Sonia Gandhi's sagacity which made her overlook the distrust her late husband Rajiv Gandhi had for the Bengal veteran.

Files Nomination Papers

Eventually, the battle lines were clearly drawn as the two presidential contestants -- UPA nominee Pranab Mukherjee and Opposition-supported PA Sangma - filed their nomination papers on 28th June.

A visibly elated Pranab, flanked by Prime Minister Manmohan Singh, Congress president Sonia Gandhi, Rahul Gandhi, SP chief Mulayam Singh Yadav, RJD president Lalu Yadav and LJP chief Ram Vilas Paswan, filed four sets of nomination papers. Union ministers such as P Chidambaram, Farooq Abdullah, Ajit Singh, E Ahamed, AK Antony, Pawan

Kumar Bansal, Ashwini Kumar were also present at the time of Mukherjee filing his nomination papers.

Four sets of nomination papers, signed by as many as 480 MPs and MLAs, including Union Ministers, Chief Ministers, Congress Legislature Party leaders and PCC chiefs were submitted by Mukherjee.

Convenor of the opposition NDA and JD(U) President Sharad Yadav was the first signatory on one set of nomination papers followed by Defence Minister AK Antony. Samajwadi Party chief Mulayam Singh Yadav and BSP supremo Mayawati had also signed the nomination papers.

As a matter of abundant precaution, each set of nomination papers had 60 proposers and 60 seconders against 50 proposers and 50 seconders as required under election rules.

As expected, UPA ally Trinamool Congress, which has decided not to back Mukherjee, was not present.

SP leaders Ram Gopal Yadav, BSP leader Satish Chandra Mishra, NCP leader DP Tripathi were among others who witnessed the filing of nomination papers.

The parliamentary affairs minister Pawan Kumar Bansal, who was to be Pranab's campaign in charge said "He will get votes beyond anyone's imagination. It is a one-sided affair. The support announced by the political parties to Pranab's candidature so far, makes it clear that he is likely to get over seven lakh votes in an electoral college of 10.98 lakh".

If eight CMs accompanied Pranab, four were present when Sangma filed his papers. But in a surprise move, Sangma found support from a former Madhya Pradesh Congress leader, Arvind Netam, a tribal leader. By evening, Netam was suspended by the Congress for crossing the line.

Elated Mukherjee

After he handed over his nomination papers to Vivek Kumar Agnihotri, Rajya Sabha Secretary General and Returning

Officer for the Presidential elections, Pranab Mukherjee thanked parties like SP, BSP, JD(U), CPI-M and Shiv Sena for reposing faith in him.

Pranab said "He is grateful to them as they have reposed faith in me to occupy the office which was occupied in the past by great stalwarts of this country, let me have the blessings of God and cooperation of all at this juncture".

Two major changes have occurred in Pranab Mukherjee's life. One, of course, is that the man dubbed as 'eternal Number Two' (for being second-in-command to three Prime Ministers) is finally poised for the top slot – the President of India.

Mukherjee has stopped getting angry, his close aides observed. On 13 June, 2012, hours after Trinamool Congress chief Mamata Banerjee tried to make the day unlucky for Mukherjee, clubbing with Samajwadi Party (SP) chief Mulayam Singh Yadav to announce their own set of presidential candidate, a cabinet colleague had asked him, "Are you not angry?"

Mukherjee smiled and replied, "I get angry only when there is no crisis. But when there's a crisis, I always keep my cool".

Poll threatens to turn murky

The Election Commission (EC) on July 4 asked VK Agnihotri, the Returning Officer for July 19 presidential poll, to show the documents on the basis of which the latter rejected Opposition candidate PA Sangma's allegation that UPA nominee Pranab Mukherjee used `forgery' to escape disqualification.

The poll watchdog's directive to Agnithotri, who is also the secretary general of the Rajya Sabha, approached him for direction on what should he do in face of the Opposition's demand to list the reasons backing his decision to allow Mukherjee to stay in the field.

The direction came amid indications of the race turning acrimonious over the charge of Sangma and his supporters that Mukherjee was ineligible to contest as he did not resign as the director of Indian Statistical Institute (ISI), Kolkata, before filing his nomination papers. They have argued that the director of ISI was an office of profit and by holding on to it Mukherjee attracted disqualification.

Agnihotri rejected the argument, but Sangma and his backers, while sticking to their charge, demanded that he must spell out in detail why he rejected their allegation to allow the UPA nominee to stay in the fray.

Mukherjee and his UPA sponsors were, however, unfazed. They dismissed the charge and pressed ahead with their plans to mobilise support. In an ambitious outreach towards the UPA dissident, Trinamool Congress chief and Bengal CM, who was not ready to back the coalition nominee, the GoM on media has decided to travel to Kolkata. Although the ministerial group has been visiting state capitals, their latest destination has assumed significance because of Banerjee's refusal to fall in line.

The BJP raised the ante by alleging that the documents, which Mukherjee cited to claim that he had ceased to be the director of ISI before filing his nomination papers, were forged, and indicated that it was keeping open the option of moving the court.

Responding to the BJP's charge, Mukherjee countered "Who had forged my signature? I myself? I do not know what they have said. Who can forge his own signature? How can somebody lodge a complaint that you forged your own signature?"

"All these issues have been represented by my authorised representatives before the returning officer... and the RO has responded to that," said Mukherjee.

Mukherjee's poll managers claimed they have drawn up a strategy to counter "frivolous objections" to his candidature.

Alleging that the resignation letter was prepared at the last minute only to save his nomination, BJP asked Mukherjee and eminent scientist MGK Menon, who is the president of ISI, to come clean on the issue.

Satyapal Jain, head of party's legal cell and Sangma's counsel indicated that party could move court: "All options are open... election petition can be filed after the declaration of result... we will cross the bridge after receiving the copy of order on NDA's plea against Mukherjee," he said.

Accusing UPA of "lowering the dignity" of the post of President, Jain said, "election petition is the only remedy once the results are declared".

In Mukherjee's defence, Home Minister P Chidambaram described as "scandalous" BJP's contention that his resignation letter to the ISI was forged. "It is a scandalous suggestion and I am sure Pranab Mukherjee has taken note of this scandalous statement," he told.

Congress said BJP should not treat President's post like students' union of a university, terming as "scandalous" the charge that Pranab Mukherjee forged his own signature to resign from the ISI.

AICC spokesman Manish Tewari said, "Sangma and his supporters should seriously think this is not a university students' union election. It is the election for the President of India. They should act as per the dignity of the high office".

Parliamentary affairs minister Pawan Bansal rubbished charges that Mukherjee resigned on a "backdate" as an afterthought to the objection raised by Sangma. "The moment we told him about the objection, Mukherjee opened a briefcase and handed us a copy of the resignation. BJP's charge is preposterous," he said. He added that Mukherjee has clearances like no-dues from various institutes and ministries in anticipation of objections.

Left Split

After NDA, the Left Front was split down over supporting Congress candidate Pranab Mukherjee for the President's post. CPM and Forward Bloc decided to vote for Mukherjee, but CPI and RSP decided to abstain from the presidential election to be held on July 19. The Left parties have 5 per cent votes in the 4,896-member electoral college.

After an hour-long meeting at CPM headquarters in Delhi, the four Left parties 'agreed to disagree'. The meeting was attended by CPM's Prakash Karat and Sitaram Yechury, AB Bardhan, Gurudas Dasgupta and D Raja of CPI, Debabrata Biswas and G Deverajan of Forward Bloc and T J Chandrachoodan of RSP.

The CPM too, was divided on the question of supporting Mukherjee at its politburo meeting. CPM leaders, especially from Kerala, were opposed to Mukherjee.

For the first time since 1996, Bengal CPM leaders got their way. The Bengal brigade comprising four leaders in the 15-member politburo led the charge. They were joined by Yechury, Tripura chief minister Manik Sarkar and K Varadarajan from Tamil Nadu. CPM general secretary Prakash Karat too, believed supporting Mukherjee would make tactical sense. Arch rival Trinamool Congress' staunch opposition to Mukherjee was an important factor for the CPM.

But a letter from former West Bengal chief minister Buddhadeb Bhattacharjee, who did not attend the meeting, strongly advocating for support to Mukherjee swung the CPM in his favour.

Karat said, "We decided to support the candidate who has the widest acceptance. Since 1992, we supported Congress candidates though we were opposed to their policies. We will continue to oppose UPA's neo-liberal policies".

Forward Bloc (FB) backed Mukherjee as it could drive a wedge between the Congress and the Trinamool. "Besides, he has the widest possible acceptance," FB leader Debabrata Biswas said.

But CPI leaders did not buy the argument. "We don't support UPA's neo-liberal economic policy. We don't differentiate between the Congress and Pranab Mukherjee. He is the architect of the policy," CPI's Bardhan said.

Though RSP has two MPs and 13 MLAs, the party decided to differ with its allies. RSP general secretary Chandrachoodan said, "It's not a question of numbers, but principles. We found it unethical to vote for candidates of both Congress and BJP. We have been protesting UPA's anti-people policies and rampant corruption".

Karat admitted the Left parties could not come to an agreement on the issue. "We also consulted non-Congress, secular parties like the TDP and JD(S) and took their views into account before taking a decision," Karat said.

This is, perhaps, the first time since the 1990s that fissures in the Left came out in the open though its leaders have been harping on Left unity as their priority.

CPI leader Gurudas Dasgupta said, "Presidential election is a political election. We can't look at it divorced from political and economic reality. When we are fighting the government on the streets, we can't support its candidate".

The Trinamool Dilemma

Congress felt Manmohan Singh could call up Mamata Banerjee and seek support for Mukherjee. The party feels because the Trinamool leader shared an 'excellent rapport' with the PM and it would be difficult for her to turn down his request.

But at the same time, Congress leaders pointed out that if she rejected the PM's appeal, it will end the alliance. "That will be a major embarrassment for us," a senior Congress functionary said. "But we are confident she will fall in line".

As Mukherjee was scheduled to visit West Bengal, for his poll campaign in the second week of July, the leaders hoped that the call would break the ice, and renew the possibility of the meeting between Ms Banerjee and the former finance minister.

Though the Trinamool chief was yet to declare her stand on the presidential polls, her party may abstain from the voting, felt Congress sources.

However, Trinamool leaders maintained, that their party would not back opposition candidate PA Sangma, as the move could antagonise the Muslims, which according to some estimate constitute 30 per cent of the total population of West Bengal.

The fear of cross-voting had also gripped the Trinamool with MPs such as Dinesh Trivedi and Kabir Suman openly hailing Mukherjee's candidature. Ultimately Mamata, who had initially opposed the candidature of Mukherjee, had announced her party's support to him two days before the election on July 19.

Shiv Sena for Unanimous Selection of Mukherjee

Giving a jolt to BJP's plans for a contest in the presidential poll, key NDA constituent Shiv Sena's supremo Bal Thackeray said in a statement published in the party mouthpiece 'Saamana', "Let bygones be bygones. Let us unanimously support Pranab Mukherjee and show the world that "*hum sab ek hai*" (we are all united),"

At a time when a sizeable section of the BJP, leading the NDA appeared to be planning to support P A Sangma in the Presidential race, the Sena chief said, "The farce that is on, for the top post of President is not justifiable. The country's prestige is at stake, for political gains. Those who have no merit are also in the race," a day after APJ Abdul Kalam made it clear that, he would not be contesting. The Sena chief also dismissed allegations of backstabbing by his party.

With Shiv Sena breaking ranks by expressing support to Pranab Mukherjee, BJP's task to ensure that NDA contests the presidential election became all the more tough. In a subsequent meeting of NDA partners to discuss the development, JD(U) too reportedly stuck to its stand that there should be a consensus on Mukherjee.

NDA Split Wide Open

The rift between JD(U) and BJP over the presidential poll appeared to grow deeper with Bihar chief minister Nitish Kumar saying the NDA prime ministerial candidate for the 2014 Lok Sabha elections should have "secular credentials" and that the coalition should declare its candidate in advance.

Though Nitish Kumar did not take any name, he was apparently referring to Gujarat Chief Minister Narendra Modi, who many in the BJP were projecting as a possible prime ministerial candidate.

The murmurs of protest within BJP, against going for a contest also appeared to be growing louder. Sources said sulking former Karnataka chief minister BS Yeddyurappa, had joined those who wanted a consensus on Mukherjee.

"While Mukherjee is a UPA candidate, PA Sangma belongs to NCP which is a constituent of UPA. If NDA has to support one of them, Mukherjee is a better choice as he has the stature and better credentials," a close associate of Yeddyurappa said, quoting the BJP leader.

BJP leaders Maneka Gandhi, Shatrughan Sinha and CP Thakur have already said, that Mukherjee should be president.

BJP President Nitin Gadkari along with LK Advani and Sushma Swaraj were some of the BJP leaders who were keen on a contest and their leaders needed to brainstorm on this issue.

The support extended by Assam Gana Parishad, came as some relief for the BJP, which was grasping at straws for allies - as the JD(U) and Shiv Sena deserted it. While there were speculations that Jayalalithaa's absence showed that she was unhappy, BJP sources rubbished them - contending that she had told Advani she was on a break. She had, instead, sent M Thambidurai, they added.

It also helped that JD(U) president Sharad Yadav, who proposed Mukherjee's name, had decided to keep away from the filing of Mukherjee's nomination. Yadav said, "Our support for the UPA's presidential nominee does not amount to backing the UPA or its policies".

Sangma attacked the Congress for not supporting a tribal candidate for the post of President.

Kickstarts Campaign from TN

United Progressive Alliance (UPA)'s presidential nominee, Pranab Mukherjee kicked off his presidential campaign from Tamil Nadu on 30 June 2012 when he met long-time friend and Dravida Munnetra Kazhagam (DMK) chief M Karunanidhi, besides interacting with MPs and MLAs of alliance partners in Chennai.

He later met Congress workers from the state and Puducherry, at the Tamil Nadu Congress Committee headquarters. In a brief interaction with media, Mukherjee expressed gratitude to all parties who had extended their support to his candidature.

Campaign in Hyderabad

In Hyderabad Pranab met Congress legislators and leaders which included Ghulam Nabi Azad in charge of Congress affairs in Andhra Pradesh, Chief Minister N Kiran Kumar Reddy, State Congress President Botsa Satyanarayan, Union Minister MM Pallam Raju and D Purandeshwari were among those present on the occasion. City based Majlis Ittehadul Muslimeen (MIM) Legislators, who are a part of UPA also met him separately.

In an oblique reference to Trinamool Congress, he said he had also appealed to those parties that are undecided, on whom to support in the Presidential election, to support him.

To a query on BJP, BJD and AIADMK-backed nominee PA Sangma's remark regarding his prospects to get elected to the highest constitutional post stating "Miracles can happen", the former finance minister said, "I don't know, I don't believe in miracles".

Campaign in Bangalore

In Bangalore, he met former Prime Minister HD Deve Gowda and thanked him for the support of JDS, which has 26 MLAs in Karnataka and three Lok Sabha members from the State.

Mukherjee recalled that when his candidature was announced, Prime Minister Manmohan Singh had rung up Deve Gowda, who "immediately responded to the Prime Minister's request".

Campaign in UP

Pranab Mukherjee campaigned in the key state of Uttar Pradesh, where the ruling Samajwadi Party and BSP leader Mayawati had pledged their support. Chief Minister Akhilesh Yadav hosted a lunch in honour of Mukherjee at his official residence. SP supremo Mulayam Singh Yadav and senior ministers, including Mohd Azam Khan, were among those present. Congress leaders, Union Coal Minister Shriprakash Jaiswal, Union Minister of State for Parliamentary Affairs Rajiv Shukla, UPPCC president Rita Bahuguna Joshi and CLP leader Pramod Tiwari attended the lunch. The former MLAs of smaller parties, including Mukhtar Ansari of Kaumi Ekta Dal and Anupriya Patel of Apna Dal also attended the lunch. The BSP and BJP members skipped the event.

Before leaving for Delhi, Mukherjee attended a dinner hosted by BSP supremo Mayawati at her residence where he met the party MLAs and MLCs.

Congress managers expected most of the voters from UP to vote in favour of Mukherjee, barring some 40 MLAs of the BJP and some MPs of that party.

Campaigns in North East

Pranab Mukherjee stated that he banked on judgment of the members of the Electoral College for the outcome of the forthcoming Presidential election.

During an interaction with the media in Guwahati following his interaction with Congress chief ministers, legislators, members of Parliament and leaders of certain regional political groups, Mukherjee said, "Outcome of the President's election was dependent on the judgment of members of the electoral college and I have full confidence in the judgment of the members of the electoral college".

"The Trinamool Congress is yet to take a decision about whom to support in the Presidential election. Their leader will decide on it before the actual date of election. I hope they will support me," Mukherjee said during an interaction with the media in Guwahati.

Regarding the debate over the need for a presidential debate before the Presidential election, Mukherjee said, "I love Sangma, but where is the question of a debate? The scope of such a debate was not there in Indian political system, unlike the United States and France. The Constitution may vest power in the President here but the power is executed by a council of ministers headed by the prime minister and they determine the policies. So, an appropriate debate can take place during general elections, but it is difficult to hold such debate in a multi-party system."

Mukherjee was in Guwahati to interact with Congress chief ministers and legislative party leaders of the north-east, party legislators and MPs. He also interacted with small regional political parties who are yet to decide on whom to support in the Presidential election.

Mukherjee met leaders of All India United Democratic Front (AIUDF) led by Badaruddin Ajmal and Congress' only ally in Assam, Bodoland People's Front (BPF). The AIUDF had 18 MLAs in Assam and one MP while the BPF has 12 MLAs and one MP.

Meghalaya Chief Minister Dr Mukul Sangma and Arunachal Chief Minister Nabam Tuki were in Guwahati to meet Mukherjee. He was slated to travel to Left-Front ruled Tripura to meet Chief Minister Manik Sarkar and other Left Front leaders.

President Post Stands above Party Politics

"The President stands above party politics. Given an opportunity, it shall be my endeavour to protect the values of this office with integrity, impartiality and the promotion of *'sarva dharma sambhav'* which constitutes the spirit and essence of our Constitution," Mukherjee said in a letter to Congress MLAs and MPs during his campaign in Gujarat. The letter further said:

"I was schooled in politics by the pro-poor commitment of Indira Gandhi and it remains my dream to eliminate the last vestiges of that terrifying affliction called poverty within our lifetime. I have been unwavering in my pursuit of this, in whatever responsibility that has come my way in all my years of public life.

I began my public life from my ancestral village in Bengal. At times like this, it is only human to admit a tinge of sentiment: my father late Kamada Kinkar Mukherjee, a freedom fighter, and my mother Rajlakshmi inspired me towards public service.

I am humbled and honoured by my nomination as a candidate for the 14th election of president of India. This office has been held by the very best of that great generation that constituted the founding fathers of independent, modern India: Dr Rajendra Prasad, Dr Sarvapalli Radhakrishnan, Dr Zakir Hussain and their worthy successors.

Any aspirant to this exalted position has to live up to the standards they set and the tradition they established to strengthen the democratic and constitutional foundation of our country over the past six decades. This I will endeavour to do with utmost sincerity".

Chapter - XII

Presidential Election

The presidential election, to elect the 13th President of India, was held on 19th July 2012. The last date for filing nominations was 30th June, and the votes were counted on 22nd July. On 22nd July, Mukherjee was elected, defeating his rival PA Sangma. Pranab Mukherjee was sworn in on 25th July, 2012 as the President of the Union Republic of India.

Election Process

In Constitution of India, Article 52 states that there shall be a President of India. The executive powers of the Union shall be vested in the President. He, as the head of a state, symbolizes the nation. However, powers of the Government are vested in the political office of the Prime Minister. The President of India is the first citizen and represents the nation and does not, therefore, belong to any particular political party. He is elected by the representatives of the people through an Electoral College.

Article 54 of the Constitution says

"The President shall be elected by the members of an electoral college consisting of –

(a) The elected members of both Houses of Parliament, and

(a) The elected members of the Legislative Assemblies of the States (including National Capital Territory of Delhi and the Union Territory of Pondicherry vide the Constitution 70th amendment Act, 1992).

Thus in the election of the President, the citizens play no direct part and he is elected indirectly by the representatives of the people, like the American President but no special Electoral College is elected, as in the case of America. Another point of difference that may be noted is that the election of the President of India is by the system of proportional representation, by the single transferable vote, as provided by Article 55(3) of the Constitution, while the American President is elected by the straight vote system.

Procedure for the Election

The Constitution provides for the election of the President by the system of proportional representatives by means of the single transferable vote. The Constitution also provides for weighting of votes in the election of the President based on two fundamental principles. First, to secure as far as possible, uniformity in the scale of representation of different States of the Union which emphasises the similarity in the status of the States of the Union. And secondly, to secure parity between the States as a whole and the Union in order to work up the idea of federal compact. For the purpose of securing such uniformity and parity the following method is laid down. This makes the Presidential election complicated.

In order to secure uniformity in the scale of representation of different States it is provided that every elected member of the Legislative Assembly (Vidhan Sabha) of a State has to cast as many votes as there are multiplies of one thousand in the quotient obtained by dividing the population of the State by the total number of elected members of the Assembly, and if, after taking the said multiplies of one thousand, the remainder is not less than five hundred, the votes of each member referred to are further increased by one. To put it in simpler words, each member of the Electoral College who is a member of a State Legislative Assembly will have a number of votes calculated as follows:

- Total population in the State
- Total number of elected members in the Legislative Assembly. Factions exceeding one half being counted as one.

The method of calculation:

1. The population of Andhra Pradesh is 43,502,708. Let us take the total number of elected members in the Legislative Assembly of Andhra Pradesh to be 294. To obtain the number of votes which each such elected member will be entitled to cast at the election of the President we have first to divide 43,502,708 (which is the population) by 294 (which is the total number of elected numbers), then to divide the quotient by 1,000. In this case, the quotient is 147,968.3945. The number of votes which each such member will be entitled to cast would be 147,968.3945/1000, i.e., 148.
2. Again, the population of Punjab is 1,35,51,060. Let us take the total number of elected members of the Legislature of Punjab to be 117. Now applying the aforesaid process, if we divide 1,35,51,060 (i.e., the population) by 117 (i.e., the total number of elected members), the quotient is 115821.0256. Therefore, the number of votes which each member of the Punjab Legislature would be entitled to cast is 115,821.0256/1000, i.e., 116

Each elected member of either House of Parliament shall have such number of votes as may be obtained by dividing the total number of votes assigned to the members of the Legislative Assemblies of the States under sub-clause (a) and (b) by the total number of the elected members of both Houses of Parliament, fractions exceeding one-half being counted as one and other fractions being disregarded.

$$\frac{\text{Total number of votes assigned to the elected members of the State Assemblies}}{\text{Total number of elected members of both Houses of the Parliament}}$$

Fractions exceeding one-half being counted as one.

The nomination of a candidate for election to the office of the President must be proposed by at least 50 electors, as well as seconded by another 50 electors. Each candidate has to make a security deposit of 15,000 in the Reserve Bank of India. The security deposit may be forfeited if the candidate fails to secure one - sixth of the vote.

Electoral Votes Party/Alliance Percentage

With the battle lines clearly drawn between the two candidates, the percentage vote shares of respective major parties were assessed as follows:-

- United Progressive Alliance (UPA): 33.2 per cent
- Samajwadi Party (SP): 6.2 per cent
- Left Front: 4.7 per cent
- All India Trinamool Congress (TMC): 4.4 per cent
- Bahujan Samaj Party (BSP): 3.9 per cent
- National Democratic Alliance (NDA): 28 per cent
- All India Anna Dravida Munnetra Kazhagam (AIADMK): 3.3 per cent
- Biju Janata Dal (BJD): 2.7 per cent

The numbers clearly were in favour of Pranab Mukherjee.

The Result

On 22nd July, 2012 after counting of votes, the election's Returning Officer VK Agnihotri announced: "Pranab Mukherjee has been duly elected to the office of President of India". Mukherjee gained 373,116 MP votes and 340,647 MLA votes for a total of **713,763** votes to win the election.

He defeated Sangma, who got 145,848 MP votes and 170,139 MLA votes for a total of **315,987** votes".

Voting Rows

Amongst voting controversies, Mulayam Singh Yadav was given a second ballot, but the election commission discounted and invalidated his ballot as it was not in the spirit of a secret ballot. Of the MPs, 15 votes were invalid, nine of which were for Mukherjee. In Andhra Pradesh, the Telugu Desam Party and the Telengana Rashtra Samiti abstained from voting, while in Kerala and West Bengal, the same applied to the Communist Party of India and the Revolutionary Socialist Party. In Karnataka, one MLA abstained. In Assam, there were two invalid votes and one abstention. In Bihar, three votes were invalid with one abstention. In Haryana, there were 8 invalid votes. In Chattisgarh, Himachel Pradesh and Mizoram one vote each was invalid. In Jammu and Kashmir, Maharashtra, Meghalaya and Nagaland and Punjab and Sikkim, there were two invalid votes each. In West Bengal, four votes were invalid.

Reactions

Mukherjee thanked the people of the "great country" and said, "I express deep gratitude for electing me to the high office". He later told the media, "I thank all those who supported me...I thank Sangma for congratulating me. I have received much more than I have given". He also said he would "protect, defend and preserve [the Constitution of India]. I will try to justify in a modest way as I can to be trustworthy". He was also congratulated by his former party colleagues Prime Minister Manmohan Singh, Sonia Gandhi, as well as Vice-President Hamid Ansari and BJP President Nitin Gadkari.

While Sangma congratulated Mukherjee he also added: "The process in this Presidential election has been exceptionally partisan and political. The public perception is certainly that in identification and projection of its candidate, the UPA did not genuinely build consensus, and that it persuaded political parties commanding major sections of the presidential Electoral College by economic and other packages...as well as inducements, threats and promises. For election to the Lok Sabha and Assembly, there is a code of conduct for free and fair elections. Such a code of conduct does not exist for presidential and vice-presidential elections...Rs. 57,000 crore were given to UP, Rs 27,000 crore to Bihar and so many other things have happened. We are meeting day after tomorrow to review the whole situation where this matter will come up for discussion". He also added that this was an opportunity lost to elect a tribal candidate as president. Congress spokesman Manish Tewari responded by saying: "Magnanimity should mark the conduct of people, who contest elections. Gritting after losing an election only endorses the proverb that grapes are sour;" its General Secretary Janardan Dwivedi added to criticism of Sangma's allegations that "I think one should not talk with such a narrow vision".

In response to cross-voting against party lines in Karnataka, as Mukherjee had support from 98 MLAs of the Congress and Janata Dal Secular, yet won with 19 extra votes and the Sangma got only 103 votes of BJP's 119 MLAs. The issue also reflected infighting within the Karnataka BJP between pro and anti-BS Yeddurappa factions.

Anti-corruption activist group Team Anna criticised Mukherjee by saying the country now had a "corrupt president".

Biocon CEO Kiran Mazumdar-Shaw said of the election: "We are making a mockery of the presidential post. This is considered the highest office in our country and should be apolitical. The president should be an apolitical appointee who has the stature and integrity that can hold the political system accountable. How can persons who are in office, holding key ministerial posts, be even eligible for such a post? This is becoming a political chess game which is devaluing this very lofty post".

Finally, the Best Man Won

It is a matter of great pride that a man of Pranab Mukherjee's political acumen and administrative skills is to be the next President of the country. His landslide victory proves that, he enjoys the admiration of political leaders across party lines, and this was reflected in the results that showed cross-voting in his favour in the BJP-ruled states of Karnataka, Jharkhand and Gujarat by the party's legislators. A man who has earned the sobriquet of 'walking encyclopedia' will be the best person to handle the 2014 Lok Sabha elections when a fractured mandate is expected.

In further embarrassment to the BJP, a day after it was found that 13 BJP MLAs in Karnataka had cross-voted in the presidential polls, former chief minister BS Yeddurappa praised Pranab Mukherjee and verbally attacked his own leaders, on the floor of the House. Yeddurappa equated Pranab with former presidents such as S Radhakrishnan and APJ Abdul Kalam. "I hold him in very high regard just as my leader AB Vajpayee. This election was not necessitated for a person like him".

Stays Away From Controversy

When asked by the media, regarding clemency petition of parliament attack convict Afzal Guru, President Pranab Mukherjee refrained from commenting on the issue saying "I will not go into value judgement. I have not assumed office yet, so it will not be right to comment on this issue".

Shiv Sena, which supported Mukherjee's candidature for president breaking ranks with the NDA, has called for the rejection of Guru's mercy petition.

The vintage leader also refused to make a comment on the mercy petition of Indian citizen Sarabjit Singh, who is languishing in the Pakistani jail. He said the mercy matter concerned another country and that its President would have to take a call on it. He said the responsibilities of a President had been enshrined in the Constitution, and before him many stalwarts had occupied the office since January 26,

1952. And he will limit himself to whatever responsibilities were enshrined in the Constitution.

Incredible Journey

An elated Pranab Mukherjee said that the media had to decide whether his journey was 'credible or incredible.' He said that while filing his nomination papers, his mother's face suddenly appeared before him. He pondered at that moment, what his mother would have thought of his winning the presidential elections. A small incidence came to his mind. In 1982 when he first became finance minister his mother had told his family that, "Pranab will become even busier now, he will hardly get any time". "What would she think now?" wondered Pranab Mukherjee.

According to the newly elected President Pranab Mukherjee his carrier in politics began in the state with a regional party Bangla Congress. His active political life started in Rajya Sabha. His approach he said has always been national because in his formative years, he had the privilege of seeing great personalities in Rajya Sabha.

Mukherjee recalled that, "Jairam Das Daulat Ram, Mahavir Tyagi, AP Jain, Ajit Pasad Jain, were all members of the Rajya Sabha then. Many of these stalwarts of the Congress party became ministers in the 1950s. Jairam Das Daulat Ram became a minister in 1950. Mahavir Tyagi and AP Jain became ministers in 1957, in Nehru's cabinet. The Opposition had Bhupesh Gupta, Pandit Pitambar Das of the Jan Sangh. I think after six-seven months, Advani ji joined the Rajya Sabha. So I had the privilege of being in the midst of people who belonged to the nationalistic fervor, which prevailed in the immediate post-independence period.

Polarisation

Pranab Mukherjee believes that polarisation of political parties sometimes, could be on issues. However on occasions he found that it tends to be on purely party politics, e.g. Congress versus anti Congress-opposition, for the sake of opposition. Opposition on issues is understandable and is healthy, e.g. whether there should be total State control on economy or not, whether the economy will be totally market-oriented without any social intervention or not. These are issues which can be debated; there can be two-three views etc. There is nothing wrong in it. But that should not lead to polarisation which will generate heat, hatred.

Leaders Greet Victorious Pranab

Leaders, cutting across party lines, on 22nd August, 2012 greeted Pranab Mukherjee for his victory in the presidential election.

Congress general secretary Janardhan Dwivedi said it was a matter of "great pride and happiness" that someone with a complete personality was going to be the next President.

He refused to make any adverse comment against the Opposition, which had indicated that it could go to the Supreme Court against Mukherjee's election.

"It is their concern who does what. On this occasion we want to proceed with a positive thinking. We also thank the Opposition that they opposed our candidate according to the democratic system," Dwivedi said.

Jammu and Kashmir Chief Minister Omar Abdullah said: "We are sure he will be a great President and the nation will benefit from the vast experience that he has gathered over his long and illustrious career. We look forward to receive him in Srinagar when he comes to see the tulips".

Union Minister Farooq Abdullah, on Mukherjee's election, said this was the "most delightful news we could get. "He was a man with vast experience and had a vision about the future of the country," Farooq Abdullah said.

Uttar Pradesh Chief Minister Akhilesh Yadav hoped the country would develop under Mukherjee's presidentship. SP President Mulayam Singh Yadav said the new President is an intelligent person and hoped his tenure would be good.

The CPI (M) general secretary Prakash Karat defended the party's support for Mukherjee. He indicated that the party's decision to take advantage of the rift between UPA allies was right. He said not a single committee in the party had opposed the decision to support the UPA candidate in the presidential poll.

The CPI (M) decided to support Mukherjee saying it should take advantage of the rift within the ruling alliance as Trinamool Congress was against his candidature. The Bharatiya Janata Party president Nitin Gadkari congratulated Mukherjee.

"Mukherjee is a very experienced person and takes everyone along with him. India's image as a democratic nation will be strengthened with Mukherjee as the President."

On PA Sangma's defeat, Gadkari said that it was well within the right of the BJP to put up a candidate in the presidential elections as the principal opposition party.

Maharashtra Chief Minister Prithviraj Chavan on 23rd August called up Mukherjee and congratulated him on his victory. Governor K Sankaranarayanan also sent a congratulatory message to Mukherjee.

Sankaranarayanan in his message said: "This is a richly deserved victory and has gladdened the hearts of one and all. The emphatic win is a testimony of your immense popularity and the confidence you inspire among people cutting across geographical and political lines".

"Due to his efficiency, decision-making capability and deep knowledge of the constitutional provisions, he is known as the living encyclopaedia of Indian politics. I congratulate him for this success on behalf of the entire State," Chavan said.

"Despite having held positions in the top echelons, he is very sensitive to the needs of the common man," he said.

Sangma moves Apex Court

The defeated NDA candidate, PA Sangma, on 21st August, 2012 moved the Supreme Court challenging the election of Pranab Mukherjee as President, contending that he was holding offices of profit and hence not eligible to contest for the post.

The petition, filed through counsel PV Yogeswaran, said Mukherjee was holding an office of profit, as Chairman of the Indian Statistical Institute, Kolkata, "on the date of filing his nomination; date of scrutiny as well as the date of declaration of his election as President and he continues to hold the post".

Sangma alleged that the letter of resignation of Mukherjee from the post had been fabricated and the signatures affixed by someone else. Mukherjee was also holding another office of profit, as leader of the Congress in the Lok Sabha, for the person holding this office was entitled to various facilities, in addition to what was available to him as MP.

"That the very act of bringing the said two offices… within the purview of the Parliament (Prevention of Disqualification) Act, 1959 is in itself sufficient declaration that both are offices of profit," the petition said.

"Even otherwise, the facilities to which the holder of these two offices is entitled, the nature of functions as well as the incompatibility and conflict of interest of these two offices with the office of President of India make it absolutely clear that they are, in fact, offices of profit".

The objections against Mukherjee's nomination were rejected by the Returning Officer, who did not decide the issue of genuineness of the signatures on his purported resignation from the post of ISI Chairman, Sangma said. He sought a declaration that the election of Mukherjee should be set aside and that he should be duly declared President. However, the Hon'ble Supreme Court on 5th December, 2012 dismissed PA Sangma's petition.

Redefining the Presidency

Pranab Mukherjee, is a man conscious of his political stature, yet also a realist. It's the combination of these two qualities, which, in all probability will come to define his presidency. As a skilled practitioner of statecraft, it's not surprising that "*Arthashastra*" is his favourite book, and a picture of its author, Kautilya adorns his room.

Pranab Mukherjee has also demonstrated a rare ability to read the writing on the wall. This was evident in his agreeing to work under Prime Minister Manmohan Singh, which, given his seniority and experience, could not have been easy. As Finance Minister in the early eighties, Mukherjee had signed the order appointing Manmohan Singh as the RBI Governor. Yet he stood solidly behind the PM as Singh increasingly resorted to running the government through GoMs and EGoMs, most of them headed by Mukherjee. He showed this realism once again in 2012, accepting that he wouldn't be able to become prime minister, and turned his attention to Raisina Hills.

Presidents come and go every five years. Each Rashtrapati has defined his presidency. R Venkataraman saw his presidency as an "emergency light" which automatically came on in a crisis and went off after it was over. KR Narayanan saw himself as 'working' president, while APJ Abdul Kalam was the 'People's President'.

How will Pranab Mukherjee fashion his presidency? Will his tenure be like that of the first president, Rajendra Prasad, who enjoyed a parity of stature with the then PM Jawaharlal Nehru and counselled the government on a host of issues? But, while Rajendra Prasad often volunteered advice, even unsolicited, to Nehru, Manmohan Singh is likely to informally seek Pranab Mukherjee's advice himself. There are a thousand informal ways for a President to help the Prime Minister.

The extent to which Pranab Mukherjee will be able to act as a friend, philosopher and guide to the government, and even troubleshoot behind the scenes, will depend on the kind of working relationship he and Manmohan Singh are able to establish in their new roles. Mukherjee isn't likely to be a rubber stamp President. Neither does the Constitution expect the 'Rashtrapati' to be one. At the same time, Mukherjee isn't going to be an adventurist, controversy courting President. Essentially a believer in the system, Mukherjee will be a constitutionally correct President, probably an active and interactive one too. Having been used to a 16-hour working day, he is unlikely to confine himself to 'Rashtrapati Bhawan's lawns. But he will also be watched by his erstwhile party to see whether he interferes in government decisions, given his familiarity with its functional details.

The more interesting question is whether, as the head of state, the commander in chief of the armed services, and Visitor to central universities, Mukherjee will try and restore health to our democratic institutions, which have taken a severe beating. He may not have executive powers, but will he use his position to persuade, restrain, counsel and encourage without getting into a confrontation, to move in the right direction? That remains to be seen.

Chapter - XIII

Embarks on a New Journey

Pranab Mukherjee is probably one of the most politically savvy persons to be elected to the office of the President of India. But nobody is sure of how he might act in the event of a hung Parliament during the 2014 general elections, if he suddenly becomes the supreme arbiter of power, in a fractured polity. Will he come into his own at long last, or will he prove to be yet another loyal Congressman?

Pranab Mukherjee has said, "I was present, in the Congress Working Committee of every Congress Party President, since Indira Gandhi, Narasimha Rao, Sitaram Kesri and Sonia Gandhi. Each trusted me and gave me many responsibilities. Barring a short gap of 4-5 years, I served the working committee from 1978, until my resignation from the party, ahead of the presidential polls. Each president has his or her own style of functioning. But I am unable to comment; comparing and contrasting national leaders is the job of the media in the short term and of historians in the long run".

The new President feels, "Constitutionally, the administration is transacted in the president's name, but power is vested in the prime minister and the cabinet.

The roadmap is pretty clearly drawn. There have been 12 presidents before me. The roadmap was drawn by Babu Rajendra Prasad, Sarvepalli Radhakrishnan and Zakir Hussian."

The new President said "He has received much more from the people of this great country than he has given, and now they have entrusted me with the responsibility to protect the Constitution as President of the Republic".

Mukherjee's elated supporters danced to the beat of drums and set off firecrackers outside his home as the Prime Minister Manmohan Singh and Sonia Gandhi, the Congress party chief, arrived to congratulate him. Ever since his candidature was announced by the ruling United Progressive Alliance (UPA), which is led by the Congress party, he has been the front-runner in the presidential race.

The victory was expected based on two combinations: first, the UPA has Electoral College majority, and second, Pranab Mukherjee's personality played a role. He has been a minister for such a long time that he holds a lot of IOU vouchers from a long list of politicians.

While largely a ceremonial role, the president is the supreme commander of the armed forces, oversees the formation of a government every time a new Lok Sabha is elected. His role in the government formation becomes critical in the event of a hung Parliament. In rare circumstances he can send some bills back to lawmakers for reconsideration.

Starts New Innings

Ahead of taking oath, Pranab paid tribute to Mahatma Gandhi, Jawaharlal Nehru, Indira Gandhi and Rajiv Gandhi by visiting their memorials. Dressed in a formal black achkan and churidar, Mukherjee visited Rajghat, Shanti Van as well as Shakti Sthal and Veer Bhumi.

He was administered the oath of office by Chief Justice of India SH Kapadia in the Central Hall of Parliament on 25th July, 2012 at 11.30 am.

Pranab Mukherjee took the oath in the name of God that he will faithfully execute the office of President of the Republic of India, and will to the best of his ability preserve, protect and defend the Constitution and the law, and that he will devote himself to the service and well-being of the people of the Republic of India.

After taking oath, Mukherjee exchanged chairs with President Pratibha Patil - the first woman Head of State of the country.

President Mukherjee was then given a 21-gun salute.

The oath-taking ceremony was attended by Prime Minister Manmohan Singh, UPA chairperson Sonia Gandhi, Cabinet ministers and other dignitaries. President Mukherjee's family along with other relatives from West Bengal were also present in full strength, to witness Pranab Mukherjee occupy the highest constitutional chair of the country.

The three Service Chiefs were also present to witness the 77-year old veteran of many a political battle taking over as the Supreme Commander of the Indian Armed Forces.

Mamata Banerjee, the West Bengal Chief Minister had congratulated Mukherjee over telephone after his victory over PA Sangma. Mukherjee had requested her to attend his swearing in function as President on July 25. Mamata accepted his request, and was present at the swearing in ceremony with TMC leaders - Kunal Ghosh, Derek O Brien and Mukul Roy.

Inaugural Address

Addressing the gathering in the Central Hall after swearing in, President Mukherjee said he was deeply moved by this high honour. He would protect and defend the Constitution not just in letter but also in spirit.

He also stressed on focusing overall developments in order to achieve progress. "Our job is to work; results will automatically come," Mukherjee said.

Amid several rounds of applause, Pranab Mukherjee said, "I will stay impartial during the discharge of my duties as President and ensure that even the poorest of the poor feel that they are part of this great nation". He said education has the capability to take India to a golden era.

Recalling his humble beginning in his native state West Bengal, Presidet Pranab Mukherjee said, "Trickle down theories doesn't address legitimate aspirations of the poor. We must erase poverty from the dictionary of modern India".

While hailing the valour and conviction of the Indian armed forces, President Mukherjee also the Supreme Commander of the Armed Forces said," We are in the midst of a fourth world war; the third was the Cold War, but it was very warm in Asia, Africa and Latin America till it ended in the 1990s".

War against Terrorism

"The war against terrorism is the fourth; and it is a world war because it can raise its evil head anywhere in the world," the President said in his acceptance speech in the Central Hall of Parliament.

India has been on the frontlines of this war long before many others recognized its vicious depth or poisonous consequences, he said.

He further said "He is proud of the valour, conviction and steely determination of our armed forces as they have fought this menace on our borders; of our brave police forces as they have met the enemy within; and of our people, who have defeated the terrorist trap by remaining calm in the face of extraordinary provocation".

Noting that the people of India have been "a beacon of maturity through the trauma of whiplash wounds", he reminded those who instigate violence and perpetuate hatred that "few minutes of peace will achieve far more than many years of war".

"India is content with itself, and driven by the will to sit on the high table of prosperity. It will not be deflected in its mission by noxious practitioners of terror," the President said.

Mukherjee then travelled to his new residence, Rashtrapati Bhavan, from Parliament House along with Pratibha Patil, the former President. At Rashtrapati Bhavan, President Mukherjee was given an inter-services guard of honour.

Need to ensure India free from poverty

President Pranab Mukherjee called for making Indian economy a launching pad for the "second freedom struggle" to eradicate hunger, disease and poverty.

In his first address to the nation on the eve of Independence Day (14th August, 2012), he also said that inflation, particularly high food prices, remains a cause of worry and several gaps are yet to be bridged in this growth story, including in the areas of infrastructure and agriculture.

Mukherjee said there is a need to fast-track the creation of high quality infrastructure and to extend green revolution across the country.

"Notwithstanding the tremendous pressure of an adverse external environment, our economy today is more resilient and confident. Yet there are several gaps that need to be bridged.

"Green revolution has to be extended to the eastern region of our country. Creation of high quality infrastructure has to be fast tracked. Education and health services have to reach the last man at the earliest. Much has been done, a lot more remains to be done," he said.

Mukherjee further said that "two decades of steady economic reforms have contributed to improvement in average income and consumption levels in both rural and urban areas.

"There is new found dynamism in some of the most backward areas, bringing them into national economic mainstream. If our economy has achieved critical mass, then it must become a launching pad for the next leap. "We need a second freedom struggle; this time to ensure that India is free for ever from hunger, disease and poverty".

Recalling the earlier times of the Indian economy, Mukherjee said the average annual growth rate was just one per cent between 1900 and 1947.

However, a quantum leap forward has taken the current growth rate to over 8 per cent. "... today, despite two great international crises that rocked the world and some domestic dips, we have posted an average growth rate of more than 8 per cent over the last seven years," he said.

He said that leaders like Subhas Chandra Bose and Pandit Jawaharlal Nehru believed that "free India would become, by example, an alternative model for a post-colonial world through economic equity and a social revolution inspired by harmony between communities that had been misled into hostility".

"I am not a pessimist; for me, the glass is always half full, rather than half empty. I would go to the extent of saying that the glass of modern India is more than half full," he said, while lauding the country's working class, farmers, industrialists from private and public sectors and politicians among others.

Shrugging off concerns that environment protection was coming in the way of economy's growth, Mukherjee said he did not believe that there was any inherent contradiction in protecting environment and economic development.

"As long as we heed Gandhiji's great lesson: there is sufficient in the world for man's need but not for man's greed, we are safe. We must learn to live in harmony with nature. "Nature cannot be consistent; we must be able to conserve her bounty during the many seasons of plenty so that we are not bereft during the occasional bout of scarcity," the President said.

Stress on economic equity

For real development to be achieved, "the poorest of our land must feel that they are part of the narrative of rising India," Pranab Mukherjee said to a burst of clapping, shortly after he was sworn in as the 13th President on July 25, 2012 in the historic Central Hall of Parliament. In a brief acceptance speech, Mukherjee placed "economic equity" above all the basic "fundamentals" of a modern nation – democracy, secularism, equality of every region and language and gender equality.

As he expanded on the theme of eliminating poverty, it did not go unnoticed among the gaggle of Ministers, Governors, Chief Ministers and MPs who packed Central Hall that Mukherjee, dressed in a black achkan and white churidar, took a gentle swipe at the economic reformers whom he left behind in the government that he was part of till recently: "Trickle-down theories do not address the legitimate aspirations of the poor," he stressed.

A cohesive front

The coronation day's political highlight was that even the warring elements of the United Progressive Alliance were present at the half-an-hour-long ceremony, presenting a cohesive front, a tribute to Mukherjee. While Nationalist Congress Party chief and Union Agriculture Minister Sharad Pawar sat in the front row, flanked by Ministers AK Antony and P Chidambaram, two seats away from Prime Minister Manmohan Singh, Trinamool Congress supremo and West Bengal Chief Minister Mamata Banerjee chose to sit, along with party colleagues, at the back, rather than towards the front, along with other Chief Ministers.

But as the newly sworn in President walked down the central aisle of Central Hall, in procession, at the end of the ceremony, Ms Banerjee rushed out and positioned herself to congratulate him. Mukherjee stopped, smiled and returned the greetings.

Guardian of statute

In his speech, Mukherjee touched on all the contemporary themes, terrorism, need to universalise education and elimination of corruption. "Corruption is an evil that can depress the nation's mood and sap its progress," he said adding, "We cannot allow our progress to be hijacked by the greed of a few".

But he also underscored the fact that his primary task was being the custodian of the Constitution: "The principal responsibility of this office is to function as the guardian of our Constitution. I will strive, as I said on oath, to preserve, protect and defend our Constitution not just in word but also in spirit," he said. Acknowledging that the honour of becoming President "exalts the occupant of this office," he stressed that it also "demands that he rises above personal or partisan interests in the service of the national good".

When protests become endemic we are flirting with chaos

The President's comments against the backdrop of anti-corruption protests of Anna Hazare and Baba Ramdev came obliquely in his maiden address to the nation on the eve of 66th Independence Day.

In a speech that covered India's emergence as a stable democracy and its economic growth post-Independence, the new President also warned that if progress fell behind rising aspirations of the youth "rage will manifest".

Earlier last month in his acceptance speech after his election to the post, Mukherjee had said that trickledown theories do not address the legitimate aspirations of the poor.

In his address, he said if Indian economy has achieved critical mass, then it must become a launching pad for the next leap. "We need a second freedom struggle; this time to ensure that India is free for ever from hunger, disease and poverty".

Mukherjee said, "anger against the bitter pandemic of corruption is legitimate, as is the protest against this plague that is eroding the capability and potential of our nation... There are times when people lose their patience but it cannot become an excuse for an assault on our democratic institutions," he said without referring to either Anna Hazare or Baba Ramdev.

The President, a veteran parliamentarian, said the institutions were the visible pillars of the Constitution and if they crack, then the idealism of the Constitution cannot hold.

"They are the interface between principles and the people. Our institutions may have suffered the weariness of time; the answer is not to destroy what has been built, but to re-engineer them so that they become stronger than before. Institutions are the guardians of our liberty," he said. Asserting that legislation cannot be taken away from legislature, Mukherjee said the people have a right to express their discontent.

"But we must also understand that legislation cannot be wrenched away from the legislature or justice from the judiciary".

The President said when authority becomes authoritarian, democracy suffers; "but when protest becomes endemic, we are flirting with chaos".

"Democracy is a shared process. We all win or lose together. Democratic temper calls for dignity of behaviour and tolerance of contrary views. Parliament will live by its own calendar and rhythm... Sometimes that rhythm sounds a bit atonal; but in a democracy there is always judgement day, an election. Parliament is the soul of the people, the 'Atma' of India. We challenge its rights and duties at our peril," Mukherjee said.

He said he was saying this not in a spirit of admonition but as plea for greater understanding of existential issues that lurk behind the mask of the mundane.

"Democracy is blessed with a unique opportunity for redress of grievance through the great institutions of accountability -- free elections," Mukherjee said.

The President said the young thirst for knowledge that will lift their skills; and for opportunity that will put India on the fast track to the first world.

"They have the character; they need the chance. Education is the seed; and economy is the fruit. Provide good education; disease, hunger and poverty will recede. As I said in my acceptance speech, our motto must be: All for knowledge and knowledge for all. Vision cannot be an open-ended vista; it must be focused on our youth," the President said.

A Busy First Day as President

Known to be a workaholic, Pranab Mukherjee had a tight schedule on July 26, 2012 on the first working day of his Presidency holding a series of meetings and receiving Vice President Hamid Ansari at the Rashtrapati Bhavan.

The day for 77-year-old president Mukherjee began with a meeting with the officials of the Rashtrapati Bhavan during which he was briefed by outgoing Secretary Christy Fernandez. Fernandez's successor Omita Paul was also present at the meeting.

The new President was given a brief overview of the functioning of various departments of the Presidential Secretariat. He was a keen listener when officers from various departments gave their briefing.

This was followed by Vice President Hamid Ansari and Leader of Opposition Sushma Swaraj calling on him.

Governors Ram Naresh Yadav (Madhya Pradesh), BL Joshi (Uttar Pradesh) and K Rosaiah (Tamil Nadu) also called on Mukherjee in the forenoon.

In the afternoon, Defence Minister AK Antony had a meeting with the President, who is also the Supreme Commander of the Armed Forces. Governors of Punjab, Nagaland, Uttarakhand and Meghalaya also met the President in the evening.

Comments on Pranab's elevation

A Level-headed Person

On the joyous occasion of the President Pranab Mukherjee's coronation day, I am delighted to join his many friends and admirers in felicitating him warmly.

Pranab Mukherjee's multi-faceted personality, reflects his qualities of head and heart, and the sagacity and dedication he has brought to every public office and cabinet portfolio he has held. Despite falling age (77-year-old), his energy remains undimmed, as does his quick and lucid mind and his tireless capacity for work.

— *Sonia Gandhi,*
Congress President

A Great Statesman

It gives me great pleasure to convey my greetings to the 13th President Pranab Mukherjee. Pranabji comes from a political family of freedom-fighters but he started his career as a teacher, much as I did in the sixties.

There are few politicians who have as much knowledge and experience of parliamentary affairs as he does. My own association with him goes back many decades. During that period I have always sought to benefit and learn from his wise counsel, his vast administrative and political experience and his clarity of thought. I think that the smooth conduct of the coalition government and the completion of its full term owes greatly to Pranabji's political sagacity and stature that kept the coalition running and also to the indelible mark he left on all affairs of State, whether they related to foreign affairs, economic policy or defense and security.

Pranabji is one of those rare individuals who combine wisdom and deep thought with capacity for decision-making and action. I cannot think of anyone who is better able to reconcile the many contradictory and conflicting interests that invariably come to bear on any important national issue. His ability to bring about consensus and forge ahead is partly because of the very high esteem in which he is held by all leaders and parties across the political spectrum. Above all, he is the most outstanding and highly respected public figures of our generation.

– Dr Manmohan Singh,
Prime Minister of India

Strong partner to America

I want to congratulate President Mukherjee on his swearing-in as the 13th President of India. President Mukherjee has been a strong partner to America and the American people, working throughout his career to deepen our cooperation on a wide range of issues. I look forward to continuing to work with the government and people of India. Together we will build on our shared democratic values, strengthen this relationship even more and create a brighter future for both our people.

– Hillary Rodham Clinton,
Secretary of State, Washington, DC

A Great Patriot

Pranab Mukherjee is a wonderful statesman and a distinguished patriot. When we worked together as foreign ministers, Pranab was a committed partner in our efforts to combat terrorism, support democracy, and strengthen Indo-US ties. Having held just about every senior government position in India and having advised several international economic institutions, Pranab brings an invaluable perspective to difficult policy issues. I am grateful to his leadership, and I am glad that I will always be able to call him my friend.

– Dr Condollezza Rice,
Former United States Secretary of State

Man with Equable Temperament

I always found Pranab Babu to be a person with greatly amiable temperament and friendly nature. Those who are in parliamentary politics, all of them, have come to know him, particularly over the past few years. They all know him as an established leader of the House and an extremely efficient and competent minister. Although he has been occupying such high and important portfolios for so long, he hardly has any airs. He is a man with equable temperament. He is a man with humble political origin but someone who has made tremendous contributions and someone who has reached a height in his own rights and merits. He is not there because of his family connections or something else but for his political and administrative acumen. He has all along been loyal to his ideologies and to his party and its leadership. When I was the Speaker, he was the leader of the House. And I have always appreciated his help and assistance since then. From that point of view I have great admiration for him.

– *Somnath Chattertjee,*
Former Speaker of Lok Sabha

Capable to Shoulder Responsibility

Ever since I was introduced to Pranab Mukherjee I have always appreciated his abilities, his strength and his capability to shoulder responsibility. Sometimes I think, had Pranab not been there what would happen to this government. Whenever there is a crisis, he is there.

– *LK Advani,*
Senior *BJP leader*

A Complete Politician

Pranab Da is a glorious exception in our national political arena. He has been extremely active at the highest level of our national politics, dependable too for so many years. That itself is a rare achievement.

Pranab Da withstood all pulls and pressures of life, crossed many a hurdle to reach newer heights and rise to where he is today.

Unlike most others, Pranab Da's style of politics is not through moving around in the districts, holding street-corners, getting engaged in local organisations, party or state politics. His capital or real assets are his intellect, scholasticism and pragmatism. At times he looks more like a teacher than a political leader.

– *Mamata Banerjee,*
Chief Minister of West Bengal

A great Strategic Thinker

Right from the time I first met him I have always found him forthright, reliable and a good friend. Whenever his name comes up you think of a politician with a great intellect who is a great Indian and a great thinker.

His greatest contribution to India has been his steadfastness, his capacity for thought, and his ability to get along with people—both in India and abroad. That is what has made him such a successful Minister, whether in Finance, Foreign affairs or any other ministry.

The Rt Hon Lord Swraj Paul *of Marylebone,*
PC Deputy Leader, House of Lords

A Strong Positive Thinker

A Strategic Thinker - Right from the Day One I was quite impressed with his approach to life. The more I started to know the person, the greater was the admiration. He is a strong positive-thinker—truly rare and wonderful. He has all along been very humble and extremely positive. These two are the rarest of the rare qualities, particularly in a person of Pranab Babu's stature. At one point of time he was holding two or three crucial responsibilities he always performs two-three or even four person's job single-handedly. And he does that faultlessly.

– *RP Goenka,*
Chairman Emeritus RPG Group

Better as a FM than not as a Finance Minister

Personally I feel no one is perfect. And Pranab is no exception. He may have his imperfections, but if you ask me, I would say, on the whole, he has been a very good Finance Minister. True, he has held several important ministerial portfolios at the Centre, but to me he has been a good FM. He has all along been better as a FM than not as a Finance Minister.

— *Russi Modi,*
Former Chairman-cum-Managing Director, Tata Steel

Vigour, Clarity and Strategic Awareness

When I was just 18, I met a young political scientist who had chosen to leave his comfortable teaching position to take a plunge into the politics. He joined a new political party — Bangla Congress - a party which was still struggling through unchartered waters. My late father spoke fondly of this energetic young intellectual with a strong Congress lineage. He saw in Pranab Mukherjee the sparks of a promising political career.

Cut to 1971, I was a mere lecturer at IIT, Delhi. Unexpectedly, Pranab da called on the phone. He had heard that a Harvard returned Professor, teaching in my department at IIT, had written a book that is creating a stir among economics and discerning parliamentarians. The book apparently claimed that India can generate ten per cent rate of growth of GDP at a time when we were growing a mere three per cent. The professor claimed that the country could achieve this without foreign aid and even more, produce the atom bomb as a deterrent. Pranab da, with his indomitable spirit to pursue out-of-the-box ideas and new paradigms, was keen to meet this nutty Professor. FICCI had organized a live televised debate before an NDA budget between Yashwant Sinha, the then Finance Minister. Honestly, I was little nervous that without the official briefs and support, how would Dada challenge Yashwantji's perspectives. Well, it is then that I realized that Pranab Mukherjee has a photographic memory of advanced statistics, going back to decades. Blow by blow, it was a scintillating hour that still remains a mile stone on debates over the National Budget.

Now, I turn to two major legacies of Pranab Mukherjee that still remain unfinished. As the External Affairs Minister of India, he had a dream as to how Indian mission abroad centers could become dynamic centres of economic engagement, while serving their diplomatic purpose. Very quickly, he moved the ball and discussions began to create a tectonic-shift in the mindset of our embassies and operations thereof. However, Pranab da took up the position of Raksha Mantri of India and his dream of his, hopeful, would fructify in the years ahead.

He had another vision as the Defence Minister of India, a legacy he wanted to leave behind. He was deeply concerned about the fact a huge proportion of military hardware is being purchased from abroad, keeping ourselves technologically deficient. Obviously, a super power of the 21st century cannot be reliant on so many countries of the world for managing its military hardware. Thus, Pranab da constituted a high-powered committee to address this vital issue, of which I was a humble member. It was under Pranab Mukherjee's leadership that a totally new term was coined 'Raksha Udyog Ratna (RUR). Private sector giants of India were chosen on the basis of transparent criteria by another high-powered committee. I believe, company like Larsen & Toubro, Tata Power, Infosys, Wipro, TCS, Mahindra & Mahindra, and other such high stature companies were selected for the RUR title. This was to be the first step towards empowering Indian private sector to compete shoulder-to-shoulder some day with the world's leading giants in the manufacture of fighter aircrafts, battleships, battle tanks and the rest. This too is a dream that is alive and must, someday, fulfill Dada's expectations of a self-reliant defence sector of India.

His day ends only at midnight, yet, his vigour, clarity, and strategic awareness remains as fresh as ever. I recall meeting him at 11 pm once to discuss some policy issues – the same smile, the same warmth and the same sharpness – irrespective of whether he deferred or agreed with any provocation.

– *Dr Amit Mitra,*
Former Secretary General of FICCI

Iron Sense of Discipline

My association with Pranab Babu has been long and I cherish it. It has been always cordial, I as a scientist, he as a consummate leader, over a long period of time.

One of the most enduring, extraordinarily competent, master articulator, an outstanding political leader for decades, Pranab Mukherjee turns a young 77. Gifted with a rare photographic memory, he is known to disarm his detractors with an easy but incredibly confident style. Armed with facts, logic, a faultless chronology of events Pranab Mukherjee comes out at the top. Clearly behind the enormous charm, there lies a high-ordered precise professionalism, iron sense of discipline and, of course, commitment to the country.

– *Dr Bikas Ranjan Sinha,*
Nuclear Scientist

Enormous Competence

When I was India's candidate for the position of Secretary-General, it was Pranab Da who led the Indian delegation to the General Assembly in 2006 and so spearheaded the effort to have me elected. He encouraged me to enter political life, and he has remained and invaluable source of guidance and wisdom since.

Pranab Da is unique in his enormous competence and his profound store of knowledge and insight into the workings of our government and politics, which in turn haver been instrumental in shaping many of India's national and international achievements.

It's his dedication, diligence, intelligence, astuteness, integrity, broad acceptability and an enormous appetite for hard work that has always been a source of inspiration to all. I hold him in highest reverence and admiration.

— ***Sashi Tharoor,***
Member of Parliament

A Top Ranking Statesman

I have been knowing Pranab Mukherjee ever since the early fifties of the last century when Pranab and myself began our Intermediate studies at Suri Vidyasagar College. It was in this college I developed intimacy that has remained unabated over the years. At our formative years, I could hardly anticipate that Pranab would step into politics in later life. If morning shows the day, it at least did not in regard to Pranab's career.

His elder brother Piyusda also in the same college—a dynamic leader in college politics and a very good orator—whom we used to regard as a politician of the future. But in later life Piyusda shunned politics and took to teaching while Pranab, at a certain stage of his life, entered into politics and eventually, by virtue of his talent and worth, established himself as one of the top-ranking statesman of our time.

Essentially a religious man giving primacy on virtue and traditional Indian values all his life, it appears, he has been following the traditional moral norm that man is born to work for others. He is found to be a selfless lover of work who works for no personal interest or ambition, who does not believe in empty words, but in concrete action, and hates demagogy and so-called exhibitionism.

Pranab is a kind of leader who believes in a quiet and gentleman's politics—a kind of politics requiring a highly educated mind that excels in humility, a penchant for serving the people without any self-interest and passion for work. In the post-independence period Dr BC Roy was the only political leader of West Bengal who possessed these qualities and I daresay, Pranab is the second political leader of Bengal in whom similar qualities are very much present. It may be expected, as history has granted immortality to Dr

BC Roy as a political leader, it will accord similar recognition to Pranab, my lovable Pranab.

— ***Amal Kumar Mukhopadhya,***
Former Principal of Presidency College

Powers of India's President

India's President as the Head of the State, enjoys certain powers and performs a variety of ceremonial functions. A lowdown on the Indian First Citizen's roles and powers are discussed.

Executive Powers

The executive powers of the Indian Union vests with the President, under Article 53 of the Constitution. The President has a right to be informed of all the affairs of the nation by the Government. He enjoys powers to appoint and remove high constitutional authorities, including the Prime Minister and the Council of Ministers. All appointments of the judges of the Supreme Court and the High Courts, the state Governors, the Attorney General, the Comptroller and Auditor General (CAG), and the Chief Election Commissioner and members of the Election Commission are made in his name.

Legislative Powers

The Budget Session of Parliament always begins with the President's address and if there is a deadlock in legislation process between the two Houses of Parliament, the President summons a joint session to break the impasse. Under the Indian Constitution, the government needs prior Presidential sanction before introducing legislation such as for creating a new state or changes in the boundary of existing states or even a change in its name. Also, legislation dealing with Fundamental Rights under the Constitution requires the President's consent, similar to money bills introduced in the Lok Sabha. Besides, all bills passed by Parliament need the President's nod before becoming law.

The President also promulgates ordinances or emergent legislation during Parliament's recess. The President also nominates members to both the Houses.

However, his powers are limited to the extent that he can ask the Council of Ministers to reconsider a Bill they have sent him for signing, such as invoking of Article 356. But if the council of ministers sends back the bill, the President has no choice but to accept it.

Military Powers

The President is the Supreme Commander of the Indian Armed Forces and all officers' hold their commission at the 'Pleasure of the President'. The appointments of the three Services Chiefs are made by him. The country declares war in the name of the President and also concludes peace, all from the control and authority over Parliament that the President enjoys.

India's President has wide-ranging roles to play when it comes to diplomacy for maintaining relations with other countries. The country's Ambassadors and High Commissioners are his representatives in foreign land. He also receives the credentials of diplomatic representatives of foreign countries. The President also negotiates all treaties and agreements with other nations, which are negotiated on behalf of the president, prior to ratification by Parliament.

Judicial Powers

The President enjoys judicial powers, primarily to rectify judicial errors, grants pardons and reprieves from punishments. The President can also seek the opinion of the Supreme Court on legal and constitutional matters and on matters of national and people's interest as 'Presidential Reference'.

Financial Roles

The President causes the presentation of audit reports before Parliament and is to receive the report of the Finance Commission and to act on its recommendations. The Contingency Fund of India is also at the President's disposal.

Emergency Powers

Three kinds of emergencies are envisaged by the Constitution. Under national emergency powers, the President can declare a state of emergency after satisfying that the country's security is at peril, either from external aggression or armed rebellion within. The national emergency is declared only after the Prime Minister and the Cabinet recommends it in writing.

The emergency in a state is basically political emergency, resulting in President's rule or Governor's rule, if there is a constitutional or law and order breakdown, under Article 356 of the Constitution.

The financial emergency occurs when the financial stability of the country or any part of the country is seriously affected. The President can direct a state government to observe prudence in public expenditure. The financial emergency powers of the President have never been put to test ever in the last six decades.

"A Rubber Stamp": Looking Back

The Indian president's powers are enshrined in the Constitution, though circumscribed by conventions, precedents and amendments. The president, however, names the prime minister, following an election or the resignation of an incumbent, significant in the coalition government era. He also has, to quote Walter Bagehot on the British sovereign, "the right to be consulted, the right to encourage and the right to warn". The prime minister's corresponding duty (under Article 78) is to inform the president of all decisions of the council of ministers and provide all information sought. The president can insist that any minister's decision is submitted for cabinet consideration.

Notably, the presidential oath enjoins him to "preserve, protect and defend" the Constitution and the law. The prime minister's oath merely prescribes true faith and allegiance to it. Presidents have mostly abided by their oath. The sum of the powers mentioned above, in the hands of an astute and morally upright person, is considerable.

Veteran parliamentarian Piloo Mody (1974 civil service batch) while speaking at the Lal Bahadur Shastri National Academy of Administration, Mussoorie, four decades ago, said the best address in Lutyens' Delhi was Rashtrapati Bhavan, on Raisina Hill. But it was reserved for a "rubber stamp".

Between the high constitutional pedestal where the President of India has been placed vis a vis the allegation of being rubber stamp, going by the history of past presidents, the truth lies somewhere in between. This has primarily occurred due to each individual president's personality, perception of his assigned role and functions, as also his own interpretation of the constitutional position.

Palace Intrigues

Dr Rajendra Prasad, the first and only two-term president, wrote in March 1950 to Prime Minister Nehru, enquiring if the President could act independently of the aid and advice of the council of ministers. Attorney-General MC Setalvad pronounced that, like the British sovereign, he must never do so. Indira Gandhi codified this in 1976 (the 42nd Constitution amendment) during the Emergency. The succeeding Janata Party regime ameliorated it partially in 1978 with the 44th amendment, allowing the president to return any decision of the council for reconsideration once.

Out of non-politicians, two presidents emerge. Dr S Radhakrishnan's term spanned the calamitous 1962 Sino-Indian conflict, the deaths of Prime Ministers Jawaharlal Nehru and Lal Bahadur Shastri, the inconclusive 1965 India-Pakistan war, and the ascension of Indira Gandhi. He reportedly nudged Nehru to drop defence minister Krishna Menon, and chided the newly constituted government of Indira Gandhi in his last Republic Day address in 1966. Dr APJ Abdul Kalam, mesmerised the youth with a vision of 21st century India. Besides, his adversity-to-success saga, has such a resonance, that it inspires many people even today.

To consolidate power, Indira Gandhi used the 1969 presidential election to split the Congress and eject the old guard. Her presidents, symbolised by VV Giri and Fakhruddin Ali Ahmed, reflected a captive presidency. Re-elected in 1980, she chose Giani Zail Singh, her home minister and former Punjab CM, for presidency in 1982. Despite his initial remark that he was willing to sweep floors at Indira Gandhi's bidding, he ironically left his post much strengthened.

Preceding Zail Singh's selection was a gruelling tussle between Indira Gandhi's special assistant RK Dhawan, who supported Zail Singh's candidature, and ML Fotedar, the PM's political aide, blessed by Rajiv Gandhi and Arun Nehru, who were opposed to it. The Punjab insurgency, Zail Singh's backward class origin and loyalty to Indira Gandhi favoured him, although the sulking Kashmiri lobby sought to test Zail Singh's loyalty by demanding an undated resignation letter. These fault-lines resurfaced after Indira Gandhi's death.

Assertiveness hasn't often been a presidential trait. But, as Zail Singh showed in 1987, it can be learnt.

Zail Singh first asserted himself in 1984; meeting NT Rama Rao and his TDP MLAs in Rashtrapati Bhavan, wrongly dismissed as chief minister of Andhra Pradesh by the governor, reportedly on cues from Mrs Gandhi's aides, despite the Prime Minister's reservations. NTR got his post back, a favour he never forgot.

The year 1984 was also the year of Operation Bluestar, which begun without the president's knowledge. The same year, Indira Gandhi was assassinated and the anti-Sikh riots took place, during which the president's repeated attempts to locate home minister PV Narasimha Rao were unsuccessful till late at night. He was distressed, as no president had ever been. Had he reacted emotionally and resigned after Operation Bluestar, he would have been worshipped in Punjab. Instead, he sided with the nation, rising above religion and province. This is often forgotten by his critics. After the sordid episode, he was determined to stay, realising that he was the sole buffer between a beleaguered community and a political leadership.

The repatriation of IS Bindra, the president's only joint secretary, to Punjab and RK Dhawan's purging from the PMO, indicated that Rajiv Gandhi was relying on elements inimical to the president. Rajiv Gandhi soon abandoned conventions and constitutional provisions on PM-President relations, including informing the president on affairs of the state. The president's foreign visits were frozen for two years. Calls on the president for periodic briefings ended. If Indira Gandhi held the presidency captive, her son believed none existed. It was a unique challenge.

Zail Singh waited till the tide turned in 1987. From January, the sacking of the foreign secretary, an unpopular Postal Bill allowing mail interception (on which the president sat), the Congress's electoral rout in Haryana, the Bofors scandal, the sidelining of Arun Nehru on health grounds and the resignation of defence minister VP Singh shifted the advantage to him. He rallied the opposition, commenced consultations with disaffected Congressmen, and consulted legal luminaries on the president's residual powers to dismiss a government that was covering up corruption and devoid of moral authority. This interpretation was strongly endorsed by VC Shukla, a former Indira loyalist, and Ashoke Kumar Sen, a law minister in Nehru's cabinet. To visit '*Rashtrapati Bhavan*', they bundled into a car, fearful of the Intelligence Bureau, hardly presenting the image of valiant Rajiv-challengers.

The president kept bandying the dismissal theory, to befuddle a cornered PM, and test the Congress' internal cohesion. The consensus amongst his official aides was that the prime minister Rajiv Gandhi could not be dismissed unless he lost his majority. RK Dhawan's television interview that he saw a dismissal order is delusional. No such order existed.

An alternative strategy was to bid for a second term by contesting against the Congress' official candidate, reversing Indira's gambit of 1969. R Venkataraman, who was then the vice-president, cleverly called on the president, proclaiming that he would resign if overlooked, the Congress' favourite then being B Shankaranand. Once it sensed an emerging alliance, the Congress dropped it's favourite and immediately backed Venkataraman. By the time Zail Singh's term ended, Rajiv Gandhi was not only suddenly aware of his constitutional responsibilities but even, solicitous towards the president. Constitutional balance was restored and India got a less captive new president.

Could other presidents have employed available powers differently? Fakhruddin Ali Ahmed could certainly have delayed, if not blocked, the imposition of the Emergency in 1975. VP Singh may not have rebelled, if Rajiv Gandhi had Zail Singh's counsel rather than his antagonism. Why was SD Sharma mute, and Rao somnolent, as the Babri Masjid was felled in 1992? KR Narayanan, his presidency ending, may not have written to Prime Minister Rajiv Gandhi, on the 1984 anti-Sikh riots as he did on the 2002 Gujarat riots to PM AB Vajpayee. Finally, if Pratibha Patil had got the 2G spectrum issue referred to the cabinet, would not the subsequent fracas been avoided? Bagehot said of the British sovereign that "we must not let daylight upon magic".

However, regrettably, "rubber stamps" are favoured choices. The irony though is that, once in Rashtrapati Bhavan, no incumbent can escape the daylight or his oath or his predecessors' tribulations. Quite often, the post shapes the incumbent.

The vintage Congress politician and the party's chief troubleshooter now faces the challenge to be a model President, who is Constitutionally correct, politically neutral and, yet, socially admired. President Mukherjee's high-profile political career, unlike most of his predecessors in Rashtrapati Bhavan, is expected to keep his five-year stint under the constant gaze of critics' right from the first day.

President Pranab Mukherjee's supporters are hopeful that his presence will be comforting in times of political turmoil, his detractors too expect him to uphold the propriety that defines his new office.

A BJP leader said "The Supreme Court has already laid out the norms to be followed with regard to the formations of governments and imposition of President's rule". "The days of Fakhruddin Ali Ahmeds and Zail Singhs are over. We hope Pranab babu, given his stature and knowledge, will uphold the Constitution in letter and spirit," he added.

While phrases like *"rubber-stamp President"*, *"activist President"* and *"People's President"* have often been used to describe the incumbents, none of these, fits into the role defined in the Constitution. According to the Constitution, "There shall be a President of India. The executive power of the Union shall be vested in the President and shall be exercised by him either directly or through officers subordinate to him in accordance with this Constitution... Nothing in this article shall (a) be deemed to transfer to the President any function conferred by any existing law on the Government of any State or other authority; or (b) prevent Parliament from conferring by law functions on authorities other than the President".

During his post-election media interactions, President Mukherjee emphasised, that the Constitution simply does not provide for an "active" or "passive" or "activist" President. His new job, President Mukherjee said, is to "defend and preserve the Constitution". He also said that he was going through the inaugural address of President S Radhakrishnan. The reference to India's second president appeared deliberate, given the fact that President Radhakrishnan, who is remembered as an intellectual and philosopher, left no trace of controversy in office.

However, some former presidents have made use of a critical article in the Constitution that says: "It shall be the duty of the Prime Minister (a) to communicate to the President all decisions of the Council of Ministers relating to the administration of the affairs of the Union and proposals for legislation; (b) to furnish such information relating to the administration of the affairs of the Union and proposals for legislation as the President may call for; and (c) if the President so requires, to submit for the consideration of the

Council of Ministers any matter on which a decision has been taken by a Minister".

Kin meet President seek help for Sarabjit's release

Dalbir Kaur and Swapandeep Kaur, sister and daughter of Indian death row prisoner in Pakistan, Sarabjit Singh, met President Pranab Mukherjee August 25, 2012 and sought his help in freeing Singh.

Dalbir Kaur said she told Mukherjee about the poor health of her brother and Sarabjit's apprehension about getting poisoned in jail.

Sarabjit Singh, who has been languishing in Kot Lakpat jail in Lahore, had said that there were attempts to poison him. "I urged the President to use his influence and take up the issue with his Pakistani counterpart. Mukherjee has assured me all possible help," she said.

Dalbir Kaur said she had earlier met Pranab Mukherjee a couple of times during his stint as finance minister.

Sarabjit's daughter Swapandeep Kaur said she also urged the President to ask Prime Minister Manmohan Singh to raise her father's issue during his forthcoming visit to Pakistan.

The poisoning issue in jail should be investigated and my father should be provided with best medical aid," she said.

Perturbed over Sarabjit's poor health, the family has applied for visa to visit Pakistan. "I also urged the President to use his influence in getting us visa so that we could meet Sarabjit Singh," said Dalbir Kaur.

President's Personal Staff

Amongst the first actions of Pranab Mukherjee after becoming the President was to appoint Ms Omita Paul as his secretary in place of Christy Fernandez

Now, Paul is secretary to the new President, Pranab Mukherjee, capping her long association with him as

"Madam Paul", the officer heading his team. She would have preferred to stay low-profile but attention has once again come her way given the position she enjoys.

Besides this, Pranab has appointed two private secretaries -- Rajnish and Pradeep Gupta -- both of whom were with him in the finance ministry. Suresh Yadav who was his Officer on Special Duty (OSD) in the finance ministry has been appointed as special secretary and Pradyut Guha as additional secretary.

Chapter - XIV

Vision of Developed India

Vision

Despite the hectic schedule of the highest constitutional post, the new President, Pranab Mukherjee is sure to enjoy this much coveted seat.

This is because India's top job gives him the opportunity to translate his vision into reality; that of a developed and prosperous India, which will stride ahead confidently, shoulder to shoulder with the other developed countries in the world. During his four decades of eventful and successful career in the Congress party, he served the nation in varied positions but always did his best in the interest of the nation despite the country was passing through a difficult period in the history of India. He was able to set into motion, unstoppable forces of economic growth, working along, with the then Finance Minister Manmohan Singh. And now, Pranab gets a chance again, of seeing India surging ahead, as he relinquished the post of the Finance Minister in UPA government.

Unfinished Agenda

Pranab Mukherjee has acknowledged that India and a clutch of other countries, all gained independence more than half a century ago, but the road to economic well-being that India chose, served well only in the beginning, in the first few decades. But as the decades rolled by, the system itself became a drag on the economic activity in India.

Many countries, meanwhile, went in for free enterprise and empowered their citizens to create wealth through their work, thus becoming important players in the world. A country like South Korea even joined the Organization for Economic Cooperation and Development (OECD), while India, which was once ahead of South Korea, still grapple with the poverty of its teeming millions.

Pranab Mukherjee, then being the deputy chief of the Planning Commission, seemed to have found the situation somewhat galling, and took corrective steps so that the latent talents of the Indian people could have the opportunity to blossom and be a success story, perhaps in one generation.

It is Pranab's desire, as reflected in his statements, that India should once again, regain its pride of place on the world stage; pride that the 5000-year-old civilization deserves. It is also clear from his statements that he would like Indian economic progress to be rapid, and India to achieve the developed nation status, as soon as possible.

Self-belief

For India to progress, Pranab Mukherjee is of the firm conviction that our country cannot depend on other countries. If the nation wants to make a leap, in the world as an economic power, India has to be developed by Indians, with sheer diligence, hard work and with our own investments.

He would like to usher in economic progress in the country that does not remain restricted to a few people, but reaches every nook and corner of the country. The fruits of economic progress must not fill the pockets of the rich, but must also be enjoyed by the poor and the disempowered. He would like governance in the country, to be a facilitator for development and prosperity.

Pranab believes that the best investment is that in social infrastructure and in human resources. Therefore, his vision incorporates more investments in such areas as health, education, environment and infrastructure that can lead to surer economic progress. He is all for economic cooperation with India's neighbours for mutual benefits.

At the same time, Pranab Mukherjee would like India to be a global player, to take advantage of the opportunities provided by international trade and the global economy.

Though in late seventies, Pranab Mukherjee presented a vision of youthful and confident India, eager to achieve by the dint of its own effort and endeavour, much like he has done in his own life.

Crisis Situation

It is common knowledge that when Pranab Mukherjee took charge of Finance Ministry in 2009, it was a crisis situation. Close on the heels of Eurozone crisis making its appearance, the valuation of the Indian rupee plunged to the lowest in the international market. In the present situation, it cannot regain its value in a hurry.

Despite knowing the fact that the Indian economy is in total mess, Pranab Mukherjee believed that there did exit a slender chance of reviving the economy with some hard work and some policy changes, in the next three years.

While taking the decision to take up the offer to be at the helm, as Finance Minister, at a crucial point, he delivered a greater amount of success. But his journey ended quite in an abrupt manner, when he was nominated as candidate for presidential election.

Inspirational Figure

Pranab Mukherjee is an inspirational figure. The story of his life enthuses one to strive and to accomplish, to be constantly in the pursuit of excellence. To be daring and not diffident, to have faith in the Divine, and to do one's duty; come what may.

Fortune, it is said, favours the brave. Destiny must have played a key role in giving Pranab Mukherjee the opportunity, to guide the destiny of the second largest democracy in the world. In 1991, Pranab would have been happy with a footnote in history. But fate has given him a whole new chapter to write, and as he wishes, in his capacity as the President of India.

Concerned about fiscal deficit

Expressing serious concern over fiscal deficit, President Pranab Mukherjee said if subsidies are not contained below two per cent of the GDP, it may pose a serious problem for the economy.

Fiscal deficit which is not confined to 5.1 per cent of GDP as projected in the Budget and one of the concomitant of which that we must reduce the subsidies and keep it below 2 per cent of GDP is not materialised would pose serious problems.

With the rising global prices of crude oil and hardening of other commodities, it is expected that fiscal deficit could breach the budget estimate for the current fiscal.

The major subsidies given by the Centre are for food, fertilisers and petroleum products.

Pointing that the current account deficit (CAD) of around 4 per cent is a matter of concern, Mukherjee felt, the economic growth "has been very slow, particularly since the global financial crisis".

In 2008-09, it was 6.7 per cent. 2011-12, it has recorded 6.5 per cent. The first quarter of 2012-13, it is 5.5 per cent. No doubt it is disappointing and that even when exports have slowed down, the diversification of export destinations is yielding some positive results.

President said that for slowdown of exports from previous years from records of 30 per cent growth is no doubt an area of concerns but side by side if we look at the process of diversification of the export basket commodities and geographical direction of the export destination, you will find that the picture is not totally disappointing and emphasised that he had the privilege of working in difficult economic situations and overcoming them.

"High rate of inflation, slow growth, high current account deficit, high fiscal deficit and how Indian economy and system has responded to those problems and ultimately we have overcome those problems....

".... through our own efforts and own efforts collectively of Indian entrepreneurs, Indian policy-makers, Indian workers, Indian farmers and over and above the new dynamic younger generation," Mukherjee said. He had the privilege of working in difficult economic situations and overcoming them.

"High rate of inflation, slow growth, high current account deficit, high fiscal deficit and how Indian economy and system has responded to those problems and ultimately we have overcome those problems....

".... through our own efforts and own efforts collectively of Indian entrepreneurs, Indian policy makers, Indian workers, Indian farmers and over and above the new dynamic younger generation," Mukherjee said.

Need to be optimistic

Pranab Mukherjee said that we need to be optimistic with entrepreneurial spirit to overcome the problem of high fiscal and current account deficits, high inflation and low growth. He recalled that India had faced similar economic challenges in the past and alluded that India had overcome these challenges successfully through collective efforts of different segments of the Indian economy.

Mukherjee pointed out that Indian exports have diversified both in terms of products and regions in the recent past and during the last decade Indian economy had grown by 8.75 per cent, which is higher than that of many other emerging economies. We should remain optimistic about the ability of the Indian economy to pull through the current bout of economic slowdown, he added.

He lauded CII's positive role in India's development and especially emphasised the green initiative of CII especially in launching of 1.2 billion square feet of green buildings which were launched under the aegis of CII. Appreciating the CII efforts in promoting young Indians said that young India represented magna-carta of socio economic transformation and said that younger people must be encouraged to realise the latent potential.

Index

Some of our Learned Authors

General S Padmanabhan; General VP Malik; Air Chief Marshal Fali Homi Major; Admiral Vishnu Bhagwat; Admiral Nirmal Verma; Admiral Arun Prakash; Vice Admiral Vijay Shankar; Lt Gen Arjun Ray; Dr A Sivathanu Pillai DRDO; Parvez Dewan IAS; Dhirendra Singh IAS; Kalyan Ray IAS; Sangeeta Goel IAS; HN Das IAS; Dr Surender Ghonkrokta IAS; Falguni Rajkumar IAS; G Sundaram IAS; PS Bhatnagar IAS; N Vittal IAS; PK Agrawal IAS; Sudhir S Baloeria IAS; NS Sisodia IAS; Dhirendra Singh IAS; Dr Yogendra Narain IPS; JK Bagchi IAS; TSR Subramanian IAS; Prakash Singh IPS; DC Nath IPS; Ajit Doval IPS; SP Mathur IPS; MK Dhar IPS; SK Datta IPS; HS Swan IPS; BR Lall IPS; PC Dogra IPS; DC Pathak IPS; ML Kumawat IPS; Dr. S Subramanian IPS; RK Ohri IPS; RB Sreekumar IPS; Kalyan K Mitra IPS; RS Gupta IPS; K Koshy IPS; Kuldeep Khoda IPS; Ajay Kashyap IPS; Dr N Dilip Kumar IPS; Dr Nazrul Islam IPS; Dr DV Guruprasad IPS; AP Maheshwari IPS; Loknath Behera IPS; Dr NC Asthana IPS; PM Nair IPS; Dr Sundari Nanda IPS; Keshav Kumar IPS; Dr Prateep V Philip IPS; Muktesh Chander IPS; Dr PS Pasricha IPS; VK Agarwal IRS; Virendra Gupta IFS; Lt Gen SK Sinha; Lt Gen Raj Kadyan; Lt Gen Mukesh Sabharwal; Lt Gen HB Kala; Lt Gen PC Katoch; Lt Gen Gautam Banerjee; Lt Gen Ashok Kapur; Vice Admiral Suresh Bangara; Lt Gen CK Kapur; Lt Gen NS Narahari; Lt Gen Chandra Shekhar; Lt Gen ML Chibber; Lt Gen Ashok Joshi; Lt Gen DB Shekatkar; Lt Gen SRR Aiyengar; Lt Gen Utpal Bhattacharyya; Lt Gen Kamal Davar; Lt Gen Amitav Mukherji; Maj Gen Nilendra Kumar; Maj Gen Vinod Saighal; Maj Gen VK Singh; Maj Gen Anjan Mukherjee; Maj Gen Raj Mehta; Maj Gen Samay Ram; Maj Gen Y Behl; Maj Gen GD Bakshi; Gen Deepak Kapoor; Air Marshal SR Deshpande; Air Marshal RC Bajpai; Air Chief Marshal PV Naik; Air Vice Marshal AK Tiwary; Air Cmde (Dr) CN Ghosh; Ambassador Kishan S Rana IFS; Cmde Ranjit B Rai; Capt (IN) Alok Bansal; VK Singal IRS; Sudha Raman; Brig Yash Mohan; Brig Trigunesh Mukherjee; Brig. MS Patial; Col PK Gautam; Col Arun Jha; Col MS Jaswal; Col Anil Shorey; Lt Col Anil Bhatt; Dr Harsh Vardhan; Ratan Sharda, Sudhakar Raje; Dr RK Tiwari; Anuj Dhar, Journalist; Ranjit Kumar, Journalist; SK Vikram; Gopal Chowdhuri; Dr Pramod Sharma; Swati Sharma, etc.